Generis

PUBLISHING

The Involvement of the People in Political Governance - A Liberian Dilemma

A Case Study of the National Legislature, 2006-2023

Arthur T. Johnson

Title: The Involvement of the People in Political Governance - A Liberian Dilemma

A Case Study of the National Legislature, 2006-2023

ISBN: 979-8-89248-206-6

Author: Arthur T. Johnson

Cover image: https://pixabay.com/

Publisher: Generis Publishing
Online orders: www.generis-publishing.com
Contact email: info@generis-publishing.com

TABLE OF CONTENTS

CHAPTER ONE.
INTRODUCTION

1.1. Background of the Study

Madam Ellen Johnson Sirleaf was declared the winner of the run-off elections between her and the former football star George Manneh Weah in November 2005. The end of the election was characterized by claims for Mr. Weah about electoral fraud, which many believed would affect the inauguration date, January 16, 2005. Madam Ellen Johnson Sirleaf's inauguration marked the end of the transition leadership of His Excellency Charles Bryant. The war ended in 2003 and was officially declared in 2004. At the end of the Conflict in 2003 and officially ending in 2004, President Charles Taylor was forced into exile in Nigeria. The United Nations Mission in Liberia (UNMIL) moved into Liberia and established national security. President Sirleaf was inaugurated as the first female president of Liberia. She faced severe challenges and problems in the country, which were inherited problems growing out of the long-term misrule by the governments of Liberia from the nation's formative period (Bernard, 1999).

The definition of good governance is not the concern here, but it is the basic tenets upon which it can be achieved and sustained in Liberian political governance. In this study, the clarifications and factors impeding good governance in Liberia will be made. To be exact on this subject, it is essential to stress the functions and roles of the legislature in this process. The assessments of the part of the legislature and the recommendations will also be looked at in this study—the strategy of the European Commission (EC) (Douglas, 2009).

A thorough understanding of good governance is necessary for the function of the national legislature and lawmakers in the best practices of democracy and good governance. Good governance concepts differ from the context and range of legislative goals (Office of the United Nations High Commission on Human Rights, 2004). The constant external imposition of funders hampers good governance. It is essential to realize that good governance serves the best interests of all people and that strong leadership commitment is necessary to implement these objectives at least partially (United et al., 2007). However, the concept of good governance needs to be modified for the context of Liberia (Adam, 1999).

The infrastructure and trust in Liberia must be rebuilt as a post-conflict nation. Despite having abundant natural resources, Liberia's economy is in ruins, most people live in utter poverty, and women are subjected to tyranny. The Liberian government has subpar institutions, and there is widespread corruption. It is, at best, a fledgling democracy following the 2005 national elections. With outside support and the presence of UN forces, it appears possible to maintain security and essential services. When the world determines that Liberia must stand alone, the people of that country must come up to the challenge. Through effective legislation, just and responsible representation of the people, and efficient oversight of the executive branch, Parliament and Parliamentarians, as crucial players, can contribute to the numerous duties of good governance (Coale & William, 1978).

Reflecting on recent developments in Liberia beyond 2005, such as political changes and economic progress, Liberia has progressed significantly in democracy up to 2023. In the 2023 elections, the National Election Commission of Liberia certified 46 political parties and some independents to participate in the legislative and presidential elections (World Bank, 2023).In substance, 20 presidential candidates and 100 senatorial candidates contested for 15 seats, and 900 Representatives contested for 73 vacant seats in the House of Representatives (World Bank, 2023) in assuring Liberians of the peaceful, fair, and democratic conduct of the elections, the Government of Liberia, together with political parties, signed the Farmington Declaration in meeting the standards, which was adhered to by the parties to relevant standards (World Bank, 2023).

From the economic perspective, since 2005, Liberia's economy has expanded by 4.6 % despite global challenges, such as the Russia and Ukraine wars that have depressed the economy in developed nations (World Bank, 2023). Mining and a healthy harvest drove expansion. Rice and cassava production boosted agricultural growth to 5.9% from 3.3% in 2021. Gold production moved 10.4% industrial output growth in 2022. Services growth fell to 2.8% from 3.0% in 2021 due to construction and hospitality factors (World Bank, 2023). Despite worldwide gasoline and food prices, 2022 inflation was limited. Headline inflation rose from 5.5% in December 2021 to 9.2% in December 2022, although yearly average inflation fell to 7.6% from 7.8%. Food prices fell 1.6% due to improved agricultural harvests, while non-food inflation rose 10.6% due to energy prices (World Bank, 2023). Government finances worsened in 2022. Compared to 2.4% in 2021, the deficit rose to 5.6% of GDP in 2022. IDA financing policy (particularly the fall in grants) and lower-than-expected iron ore royalties due to delayed Arcelor Mittal mining project development, expenditure overruns on goods and services, transfers, and subsidies contributed to this. A debt-to-

GDP ratio 53.4 puts Liberia at moderate risk of external debt distress and high risk of overall debt distress (World Bank, 2023).

According to the World Bank (2023), in 2022, Liberia's current account balance was high despite rising gold exports. High global food and fuel prices (Liberia is a net importer) reduced the current account deficit to 17.7% of GDP, down from 17.8% in 2021. Improved trade drove the recent account balance improvement. Rising gold quantities and export prices reduced the trade imbalance from 13.1% of GDP in 2021 to 11.8%. Project grant and loan disbursements fell, making current account deficit financing difficult despite substantial foreign direct investment (7.4% of GDP in 2022). Mining expansion and energy, transportation, trade, and financial services reforms are expected to boost the GDP by 4.5% in 2023. Ongoing mining operations and improved access to inexpensive energy and roads will increase output across several economic sectors. Inflation is expected to rise to 10.4% in 2023 due to a domestic currency devaluation and rising food prices, then moderate to 5.5% by 2025 by global energy and food prices (World Bank, 2023).

Election plays a significant role in the Liberian democratic process of governance and responsible leadership and development. Over the years, Liberia has improved significantly in the conduct of its elections (NEC et al., 2023). Women participants had declined from 2005 (which witnessed the highest number of women participation in the three branches of government) (NEC et al., 2023). Many people still doubt electoral integrity in Liberia (Birck, 2020, cited in NEC et al., 2023). In the 2014 election, 50 percent of the participants believed the polls were not credible (Liberia Media Center, 2014, cited in NEC et al., 2023, p.19). While elections of officials in offices have improved considerably in Liberia, particularly elected Representatives, there are questions about the participation of the electorates in Legislative decision-making, which remains fundamental in the body politics of Liberia to address the crisis of participation governance.

1.2. Statement of the Problem

Political participation in Liberia has always been a problem. The involvement of the people in the decision-making process has been one of the major causes of Liberia's political crisis. These problems have persisted since the formative days of the Liberian state, causing changes in governments both violently and in democratic elections. A case study is directed at the National Legislature, in which members of the Legislature and the bureaucracy in legislation are examined to determine the level of involvement of the represented people. It shows that people are unaware of the laws promulgated by their respective representatives and the extent of the nature and context of those laws passed, affecting their lives daily.

Consequently, elections of members of the Legislature are expected to be done based on formed policies and issues of national development. The question is whether voting of the legislative members is done on national issues or other personal beliefs of the electorates. The answer is that the Legislative branch has yet to have a standardized system that points to accountability and participation that the elected will be accountable for what they do and how they do it in the Legislature. The absence of this participation in the legislative process is a severe dilemma in Liberian body politics. Therefore, the problem of legislative representation in Liberia has not taken complete democratic norms; the processes and procedures leading to the election and post-election activities by the winners are seen as significant challenges or problems faced by the people. In this regard, an assessment of some of the challenges was considered.

1.3. Theoretical Framework and Assumptions

Good governance is fundamental in sustaining democracy and political participation. According to Bo Rothstein and Jan Teorell, the critical element of good governance is when political institutions' functions are reflected impartially. This also requires institutions responsible for conducting elections to be credible and impartial. Ngaire Woods asserts that participation in governance is one of the essential components of good governance when the people affected by governance are directly involved in the decision-making process of the decisions that will affect them because they will claim ownership (Woods, 1999). The theory of "integrity pillars" by Jeremy Pope states that important institutions must work together to ensure good governance and that their failure threatens it. An elected legislature, an honest and robust executive, an independent and accountable judicial system, an independent auditor general (subordinated to Parliament), an Ombudsman, a specialized and independent anticorruption agency, a non-politicized civil service, an honest and efficient local government, an independent and free media, a civil society that promotes public integrity, reliable corporations, and an international framework. This vast collection of anticorruption techniques needed prioritization based on what causes what. The precise specification of institutional designs also suggests that certain institutions and designs must lead to good governance. Since the end of the second two civil wars, Liberia, a small coastal nation in West Africa on the Gulf of Guinea, has made significant development advancements (1989-1997 and 1999-2003)—the third general election since the conflict was held in Liberia in late 2017. Former soccer player George Weah won the presidency in a runoff and took office on January 22, 2018. In Liberia's first electoral transfer of state executive authority since 1944, he succeeded two-time president Ellen Johnson Sirleaf, who was forbidden by the constitution from running for a third term. Its policy agenda is centered on four main objectives: better service delivery and support for underserved groups; economic diversification and growth; furthering the consolidation of peace and security; and more excellent governance, accountability, and transparency. Weah inherits several severe issues from the Sirleaf government, such as the lingering impacts of a deadly Ebola virus outbreak in the country between 2014 and 2016, undermining its fragile economy and health system. He will govern without the assistance of UNMIL. This UN peacekeeping organization significantly supported post-war security and governance for 15 years until the end of its mandate in late March 2018.

The Weah government will probably continue to receive sizable bilateral and multilateral aid. However, his governance and leadership track record may have some bearing on the scope and direction of this assistance. The United States and Liberia have had close bilateral connections for nearly 200 years, with few exceptions. During the Sirleaf years, relationships were incredibly close. The US State Department and the US Agency for International Development (USAID) have managed numerous post-war bilateral aid programs, particularly in health and economic development. Liberia also gains from initiatives run by other US government departments and organizations, such as the Treasury Department, Peace Corps, Defense Department, and Millennium Challenge Corporation. The post-war development, stability, and democratization trajectories in Liberia have been the subject of hearings in Congress. Congress has funded over $5 billion in post-conflict aid and support to stop the Ebola outbreak. Through the House Democracy Partnership, Congress has aided in improving ties with the Liberian legislature. The immigration rights of Liberians who are not citizens of the United States have also received support from some members of Congress, frequently those who represent politically engaged Liberian-American constituents. The post-war reconstruction program for Liberia must consider the democratization of the country's representative democracy, which encourages economic growth and political involvement. The political engagement of the electorates will be necessary for the legislature's members to contribute to Liberia's post-war development (the people). Governmental legitimacy is maintained when the populace participates in decision-making, and their opinions are considered. More support for Liberia will be evident once Liberia's international allies are confident that Liberia is on this course.

1.4. Significance of the Study

This research aims to identify research that selects political, legal, and governance challenges and their effects on policy. It will make recommendations to deal with those challenges through an Inquiry into the Involvement of the People in integration and participation. In addition to the significance of the study, the research sought to contribute to the Government of Liberia's reform efforts in improving the relationship between the elected officials and the electorates through the enhancement and the establishment of solid rapport between the legislators and constituencies. The researcher also sought to validate or invalidate the current process while thoroughly investigating how the process can be better conducted. The researcher hopes this thesis will provide a path forward for an Inquiry into the Involvement of the People in decision-making in legislative matters in their constituencies. For example, after this study and its publication, if it is identified that the problems of accountability rely on both the electorates and the elected, the book or published research will be made available to members of the Legislature and library as well as citizens in understanding how to encourage political participation is legislative governance. Efforts will also be made to make this study an academically required material for schools. Also, the recommendations from the survey will be published encouraging the National legislature about how citizens' participation can be encouraged, some of which include the findings that there must be legislative websites informing about the day-to-day functions of the Legislature; citizens should be informed about how their elected Representatives vote in the Legislature and why, and encourage consultation on a regular and periodic basis for better accountability.

1.5. Purpose and Objectives of the Study

The survey aims to investigate people's participation in legislative workings in their constituencies using the national legislature as a case study. Thus, the inquiry investigated the relationships between the electorates and their lawmakers. The specific objectives of this study were:

1. To determine the relationship between lawmakers and their constituents.
2. To examine whether the electorates are fully participating in legislative activities and
3. To identify the challenges electorates faced with their lawmakers.

1.6. Research Questions

The main research question was: How is the people's participation in legislative workings in their constituencies? The specific research questions were:

1. What is the relationship between lawmakers and their constituents;
2. How are the electorates fully participating in legislative activities? and
3. What are the challenges electorates face with their lawmakers?

1.7. Scope and Delimitation of the Study

The scope of this study was from 2006 to the time of its publication of this study, and the study was delimited to the members of the national legislature at the capitol building with the topic:

The problem of political, legal, and governance challenges and their effects on the policy of the People in Political Governance -A Liberian Dilemma in Effective Governance for National Growth and Development. Therefore, the study investigates the representation of the people in political governance in the national legislature.

To build a conceptual framework that reinforces the understanding of the problem of the People in Political Governance, the study sought to draw experiences on the role of political parties and civil society institutions responsible for ensuring the realization of good democratic tendencies.

1.8. Limitations of the Study

The study covered the National Legislature at the Capitol Building. However, several constraints on the part of the researcher, which include the willingness of respondents to dish out the needed information and as well as for the researcher to have easy access to all other essential documentation that could enhance the reliability of the data if the entire country were to be covered would a challenge. Although this may not be the first of its kind study, the researcher found it difficult to get across the entire country due to bad road conditions and security; therefore, the researcher was constrained to limit the study to the vicinity under investigation. The results of this study will not be generalized because of its subjectivity.

1.9. Definition of Key Terms

The study makes use of the following words.

After the First Liberian Civil War in 1994–1995, the Economic Community of West African States (ECOWAS) dispatched a peacekeeping force to Liberia, ECOMOG.

The Economic Community of West African States, or ECOWAS for short, is a regional political and economic association of fifteen West African nations. These nations have a combined size of 5,114,162 km2 and a population of over 349 million in 2015.

Effective Governance: Good Governance is a strategy for a government devoted to developing a system that safeguards civil liberties and human rights. Participation, Rule of Law, Transparency, Responsiveness, Consensus Oriented, Equity and Inclusiveness, Effectiveness and Efficiency, and Accountability are the metrics for good governance.

Election: The official process by which a population selects a candidate for public office is known as an election. Elections have gone as expected.

Electioneering: A politician or political campaigner's active and enthusiastic participation in election campaign activities.

Those eligible to vote in an election are collectively called the electorate.

Governance is the act or process of controlling something's direction and control (such as a country or an organization).

Involve: To have an essential characteristic or consequence.

National Development: The real money generated by a nation's economic activity over a year is the national income. It covers payments made in wages, interest, rent, and profits to all resources.

The national legislature is the body of government with the authority to enact laws, as opposed to the executive and judicial branches. It consists of deliberative groups of people who are typically elected.

The House of Commons and the Lords Spiritual, who together make up the House of Lords, are the representatives of the counties, cities, boroughs, and universities in Great Britain. Historically, the House of Lords was made up of three estates.

A parliamentary expert is knowledgeable in the formal protocols of legislative and other governing bodies.

People: A group of people who reside in the same nation and are subject to the same national authority; a nationality.

People Participation: According to this study, people actively participate in political, social, and economic activities that impact their daily lives.

Political Governance: The Political Governance Program intends to boost citizens' participation in local governance and decentralization, inclusive governance, and citizen participation in decision-making. It also strives to improve the quality and conduct of elections.

Political Engagement: Citizens' actions that impact politics broadly define political participation. Politicians and academics have emphasized the distinctive nature of democracy by highlighting everyday citizens' involvement in political matters since Pericles' infamous funeral speech (431 BC). From one place, state, stage, subject, concept, etc., there is a movement, passage, or change: change.

1.10. Organization of the Study

Five chapters organized this study. The study's background is covered in Chapter 1, which also contains an introduction that highlights critical historical features of the study, a statement of the problem, the study's aim and objectives, a list of research questions, and a discussion of the study's importance. The research will analyze the study's limitations and delimitations, the definition of key terminology, and its organizational structure in Chapter 1. The examination of pertinent literature is the emphasis of Chapter 2, and the research methodology—which covers the research method, research design, sample size, sampling techniques, study population, data collection tools, data collection procedure, and data analysis procedures—is covered in Chapter 3. Data Presentation, Interpretation, Discussion, and Analysis are covered in Chapter 4, while the Summary, Conclusion, and Recommendation are covered in Chapter 5.

CHAPTER TWO.
REVIEW OF RELATED LITERATURE

2.1. Introduction

With a population of around 4.7 million, Liberia is a tiny nation in West Africa. Its administration is still working to implement a national policy plan centered on eradicating the country's pervasive poverty, fostering long-term growth and development, and repairing the infrastructure and governmental institutions ravaged by two civil wars (1989-1997 and 1999-2003). The devastating Ebola virus outbreak (2014–2016), which caused a severe decline in economic growth rates and a 1.6% contraction of the economy in 2016, was contained economically, and the nation overcame it. Liberia, a constitutional republic with a bicameral national legislature, just finished a political transition following the October 2017 presidential and House of Representatives elections and subsequent presidential runoff. George Weah of the Coalition for Democratic Change took first place in the contest (CDC). Yes, on January 22, 2018, a well-known former professional soccer player was sworn in as Liberia's 25th president and second post-war leader. Term-limited President Ellen Johnson Sirleaf, who had served two terms, was succeeded by him (Outram, 1999).

Given Liberia's history of presidential supremacy, winner-take-all politics, and undemocratic governmental transfers, the election was particularly significant from a local political standpoint. It resulted in Liberia's first transfer of state executive power via election since 1944. The considerable development achievements and reforms that Liberia has made were at stake in the election, along with its numerous economic, social, and governance issues, such as corruption and the need for accountability for the ongoing human rights violations that occurred during the country's civil war. The preservation of benefits from the United States' post-war investments of more than $5 billion in development, security, and humanitarian welfare, as well as significant help from other donors, were also at stake. Before the Ebola outbreak, which caused a severe decline in economic growth rates and a 1.6% contraction of the GDP in 2016, such assistance, combined with substantial inflows of foreign investment mainly focused on commodities, contributed to a rapid expansion of Liberia's economy.

In a statement, the Trump administration praised "the people of Liberia on the successful conclusion of the presidential runoff election" of 2017 and congratulated George Weah on his victory, calling the election process "a historic milestone for

Liberia's democracy." The National Elections Commission (NEC) of Liberia and other vital organizations that had contributed significantly to ensuring a "peaceful and transparent contest" were praised for "administrating an orderly election process." According to the statement, the United States "continues to support the success of this historic democratic transition and the peace and prosperity of Liberia" and "is deeply committed to our historical connection with Liberia and its people" (Boas, 2001).

2.2. Liberia: Political Transition and US Relations

Since the end of the second of two civil wars, Liberia, a tiny coastal nation in West Africa on the Gulf of Guinea, has achieved developmentally significant progress (1989-1997 and 1999-2003)—the third general election since the conflict was conducted in Liberia in late 2017. Former soccer player George Weah won the presidency in a runoff and took office on January 22, 2018. In Liberia's first election transfer of state executive authority since 1944, we replaced two-time president Ellen Johnson Sirleaf, who was forbidden by the constitution from running for a third term.

The core of What's policy agenda is on four main objectives: better service provision, support for marginalized populations, increased economic development and diversity, continued peace and security, and enhanced governance, accountability, and transparency. Weah inherited several severe issues from the Sirleaf government, including the lingering impacts of a deadly Ebola virus outbreak in the nation between 2014 and 2016, undermining its fragile economy and health system. He will govern without the assistance of UNMIL. This UN peacekeeping organization significantly supported post-war security and governance for 15 years until the end of its mandate in late March 2018.

The Weah government will probably continue to receive significant bilateral and international aid. However, his governance and leadership track record may have some bearing on the scope and direction of this assistance. The United States and Liberia have had close bilateral connections for almost 200 years, with few exceptions. During the Sirleaf years, relationships were incredibly tight. The US State Department and the US Agency for International Development (USAID) have managed numerous post-war bilateral aid programs, particularly in health and economic development. Liberia also gains from initiatives run by other US government departments and organizations, such as the Treasury Department, Peace Corps, Defense Department, and Millennium Challenge Corporation. The post-war growth, stability, and democratic trajectories in Liberia have been the subject of hearings in Congress. Congress has funded more than to$5 billion in post-conflict relief and support to stop the Ebola outbreak. Through the House Democracy Partnership, Congress has aided in improving ties with the Liberian legislature. Some members of Congress have also backed the immigration rights of Liberians who are not citizens of the United States, frequently those who represent politically engaged Liberian American constituents (Okolo, 1989). Since the end of the second conflict in 2003, the United States has supported Liberia with 2.4 billion in assistance package (CRS Report, 2020). According to the US Ambassador to Liberia in the Spring of 2015, as addressed in the "Ambassador Review," Liberia and the US have had long historical ties. Still, since the bloody civil war in Liberia, this relationship has become closer than ever (CRS Report, 2020, p.24).

2.2.1. U.S. Ties: Background

With Liberia, the United States has enjoyed a close bilateral connection for almost 200 years and was instrumental in the country's founding. To relocate free African Americans and former U.S. slaves in the Pepper Coast region of contemporary coastal Liberia, contacted the American Colonization Society. These pioneers proclaimed their independence in 1847, founding the Republic of Liberia. The settler population, known as Americo-Liberians, had almost complete control of the government until a coup was staged in 1980 under the leadership of a young military commander of indigenous ancestry (Stephan, 1995).

The United States funded post-conflict stabilization efforts, generously donated aid to help fulfill the needs of those in need during battle, and assisted in mediating an end to many hostilities. To show support for consolidating a ceasefire and a related agreement ending the war known as the Comprehensive Peace Agreement (CPA), then-President George W. Bush ordered a limited US military intervention in Liberia in 2003 as then-President Charles Taylor clung to power amid a rebel assault on the capital, Monrovia (CPA). Former military commander President Taylor, who served as president in 1997 following the end of the nation's first civil war, has left office thanks to the CPA (Robert, 1990).

The Economic Community of West African States (ECOWAS) Mission in Liberia (ECOMIL), sent to Liberia in September 2003, received logistical and financial support from the US. Most of its personnel were incorporated into the UN Mission in Liberia (UNMIL), a more extensive successor peacekeeping operation launched a few weeks later. On March 30, 2018, UNMIL's mission came to an end. Although the precise number has changed yearly, the United States has contributed around a quarter of UNMIL's expenditures. Because of Sirleaf's expertise in international development, her connections as a banker and businesswoman, and her frequent cordial meetings with American officials, U.S. ties with the Sirleaf government have been friendly since the beginning of her presidency. The U.S.-Liberia Partnership Dialogue, initiated by the Obama Administration in 2013, primarily focuses on bilateral development cooperation. In January 2017, the most recent conversation under this approach took place.

The appropriations process, recurring hearings on elections, Ebola, and other changes in the nation, as well as Member trips to Liberia, have influenced U.S. ties with that country. Two resolutions asking for free, fair, and peaceful elections in October 2017 and a hearing in the US House of Representatives on Liberia's 2017 election prospects were held in September 2017. Through the House Democracy Partnership (HDP) initiative, Congress has been fostering ties with the Liberian legislature since 2006. Liberian immigration to the US has also attracted some if limited, legislative interest (Wilcon, 2010).

2.2.2 Foreign Affairs

The United States and Liberia's representatives have described the relationship between Liberia and the United States as unique; it is a historical fact that the US remains Liberia's most influential partner. In Africa, Liberia remains the most regularly aligned with the United States at the General Assembly, and one of those examples of Liberia's commitment is the vote America described as critical regarding the State of Israel, among many votes (Congressional Research Service, 2023). US firms play a significant role in Liberia's economy; the Firestone Natural Rubber Company (a subsidiary of America Bridgestone, operates the largest rubber plantation in the world's most extensive private employer (Ibid. p.1). According to the Congressional Research Service (2023), rubber counts for 95 percent of US imports (p.1). President Weah called Russia's invasion of Ukraine "condemnable, unprovoked, and unjustified" and supported Ukraine's military. See https://crsreports.congress.gov. Liberia is one of few African nations to keep all six U.S.-backed Russia-Ukraine warfare United Nations General Assembly (UNGA) resolutions (Congressional Research Service, 2023).

US Involvement and Support Relations between the United States and Liberia were tense from the 1980 coup until the conclusion of Liberia's civil wars. Relations were strengthened under President Sirleaf's tenure from 2006 to 2018 due to a substantial increase in US assistance (Congressional Research Service, 2023). The U.S.-Liberia Partnership Dialogue commenced in 2013, and Liberia's legislature is a partner of the House Democracy Partnership, which includes 18 legislatures and penalties for corruption (Ibid. pp. 2-3). According to the Congressional Research

Service (2023), in 2020, the Trump Administration imposed sanctions on Liberia's ex-director of passport and visas for fraudulent activities and on a current senator, Varney Sherman, for engaging in bribery and the Biden Administration has publicly sanctioned four Liberian officials for corruption: Senator Prince Johnson, a former rebel leader and influential senator, and three top Weah administration officials, including Weah's chief of staff (pp. 2-3). President Weah suspended three officials, all resigned without punishment (Ibid. p. 2). These sanctions officials under Liberian laws are entitled to due process.

2.2.3 US Assistance to Liberia

The United States has given more than $2 billion in aid coordinated by the State Department and the US Agency for International Development (USAID) to assist with stabilization, security-sector reform, governance, and development in Liberia since the civil conflicts ended (Congressional Research Service, 2023). Congressional Research Service (2023) asserts that Liberia has obtained extra cash from global and regional programs, aid from other US agencies, and emergency funding for Ebola- and COVID-19-related support. Liberia is a priority country for the President's Malaria Initiative and Feed the Future (pp. 2-3). It collaborates with the Michigan National Guard through the State Partnership Program. Nonemergency aid from the United States to Liberia reached its highest point in 2010 and has decreased since then; in Fiscal Year 2022, funding managed by the State Department and USAID for the country amounted to $129.6 million, with approximately 50% allocated to health aid; the Fiscal Year 2022 assistance allocation included funding for education and social services ($23.0 million), economic growth ($18.0 million), democracy and governance ($15.9 million), and peace and security ($4.8 million) (Congressional Research Service, 2023). The Biden Administration has requested $115.0 million for Liberia for the fiscal year 2024 (Ibib.pp.2-3).

In 2021, the Millennium Challenge Corporation (MCC) completed a five-year, $257 million Compact in Liberia to increase power availability and enhance road infrastructure (Ibid. p.2). The previous $15 million MCC Threshold Program (2010-2013) aimed to enhance girls' school access, improve land rights, and boost trade (Ibid. p.3).

About Diaspora Liberians in the United States, approximately 100,000 Liberians born outside the United States live there, making it the largest Liberian diaspora globally, according to US Census Bureau information (Ibid.p.3). Liberians in the United States were granted Temporary Protected Status in 1991 amid the initial civil conflict (Ibid.p.3). Subsequent Administrations provided immigration relief for eligible Liberians due to ongoing war and the 2014-2016 Ebola crisis (Ibid.p.3). The Fiscal

Year 2020 National Defense Authorization Act (PL 116-92) of the United States allowed qualified Liberians and their relatives to get lawful permanent residence status (Ibid. p. 3). From a considerable point of view, the relationship between the United States and Liberia remains strategic and traditional and has grown over the ages. Liberians believe that the relationship goes beyond state-to-state interactions in international relations.

2.3. Liberia's Civil Wars: Taylor and Judicial Responses to Wartime Rights Abuses

Most of Liberia's founding freemen were deported from the US and West Indies (Guannu, 2010a), although a few were apprehended and taken to West Africa on purpose (Holloway, 1981). Liberia's political culture and government structures resemble the US (Guannu, 1981). When the Liberian State was founded, these people of color failed to demonstrate how democratic values and their wishes for life, liberty, and happiness could be accomplished. They abandoned these ideals in Liberia (Guannu, 2010a, 2010b, 2010c; Holloway, 1981). Liberia was ruled by formerly enslaved people or males of color for 133 years under a one-party regime with penetration, governance, distribution, legitimacy, identity, and historical interpretation difficulties (Guannu, 2010c). These people became close and avoided locals under servitude.

The Liberian Armed Forces took power by force in 1980 to fix the previous regime's mistakes (Guannu, 2010c). The Liberian civil war began when the military administration repeated previous mistakes, and the country's inability to recover from the brutal coup and American-Liberian misrule, as well as President Samuel Doe's ethnic factor, led to a 15-year slaughter. According to the Rome Statute, some Liberian Civil War perpetrators committed War Crimes. The international community pushed Liberian warlords and other warring factions to negotiate to end the violence (Guannu, 2010c). The "Accra Peace Accord" established a Truth and Reconciliation Commission (TRC) to hear from Liberian civil war victims, perpetrators, and other actors about their experiences, investigate the root causes and antecedents of the conflict, analyze the conflict, and make recommendations to the political establishment.

After its examination, the TRC made recommendations. The TRC recommended a Liberian crimes court to punish civil war offenders (TRC Report, 2009). The Liberian National Bar Association's leadership and many Liberians support the TRC's recommendations to establish the War and Economic Crimes Court (Geterminah, 2021; Kionyeneh, 2021). What remains a question for the political establishment of

Liberia is whether or not the establishment of the War Crimes Court in Liberia is possible. Amid these concerns, there are some impediments to establishing the war crimes court.

The Supreme Court of Liberia in the case Archie Williams versus Christina Tah, Minister of Justice and Attorney General of Liberian and the Independent Human Rights Commission, decided in 2011, the Supreme Court of Liberia ruled that the TRC recommendation sanctioning alleged perpetrators was unconstitutional and that the recommendations are not binding but instead advises left for the President of Liberia to implement or avoid implementation. The Government of Liberia in 2003 passed into law a general amnesty to all alleged perpetrators of war crimes from 1989 to 2003 (Act of Immunity, 2003 of Liberia). The Constitution of Liberia, Chapter XIII, Articles 97 pardons all perpetrators of atrocities from 1980 to 1985 (Const. of Lib. art. 97). Since the elections of Presidents Ellen Johnson-Sirleaf and George Weah, these former leaders failed to implement the TRC recommendation and establish the economic and war crimes court in Liberia. Political reasons: The above impediments and political factors may be responsible for these presidents' failure to show the court. With the election of President Joseph Nyuma Boakai, Sr., he had promised to set up a committee to study the issue regarding the establishment of the economic and war crimes court in Liberia. This is not a clear-cut policy statement that the government will establish the war crimes court in Liberia, but rather a promise as to whether or not it is possible and should be done.

2.3.1. Political Background of Sirleaf Administration (2006-2018)

After defeating Weah in a runoff in Liberia's first general elections following the war in 2005, Ellen Johnson Sirleaf, a former government administrator, banker, and UN Development Program official with an education in the United States, was elected president. She assumed office in early 2006, taking over from the National Transitional Government of Liberia, which the people had yet to choose. She was the first woman to be elected president of an African nation. During her first term, she concentrated on moving Liberia away from rapid postwar recovery and humanitarian aid and toward a longer-term development goal. Although public services and infrastructure remain underdeveloped and poverty has persisted, Sirleaf is recognized as having gained the trust of international aid donors, which has resulted in significant, ongoing infusions of money for the nation torn apart by conflict. Along with several other development and stabilization initiatives, this aid-funded infrastructure restoration and the development of governmental and institutional capacity (Samuel, 2009).

The national budget increased from $80 million in 2006 to $516 million after her first term, thanks to rising state income. During her leadership, Liberia also formed a Truth and Reconciliation Commission. Many of its suggestions needed to be more contentious and partially adopted. One of its recommendations called for the exclusion from public leadership positions of Sirleaf and other individuals who were the most vocal critics or accused leaders of armed civil war factions. The USAID-run Governance and Economic Management Program provided the Sirleaf government with much monitoring and support (GEMAP, 2005-2010). It supported efforts to strengthen judicial ability and encourage varied economic governance by enhancing state budgetary management and contracting capacities and combating administrative corruption. However, local sovereignty-focused complaints were leveled at employing contract-based foreign managers to oversee the financial flows of crucial public sector revenue-earning organizations. The Governance and Economic Management Support (GEMS) program, a similar follow-up initiative, ended in 2016. In a fiercely contested runoff election in 2011, Sirleaf defeated Winston Tubman of the Congress for Democratic Change party, whose vice-presidential candidate was Weah. As Sirleaf's second term went on, domestic criticism of her performance as a leader increased. Critics, including the numerous opposition parties in the country, claimed that she had fallen short of fulfilling her campaign promises regarding improving living standards, job growth, and service delivery. Another area of criticism was the corruption in her government. Even though Sirleaf was not charged with a crime and made several steps to address the issue, her administration frequently found itself at the center of controversies involving its staff. Because three of her sons were appointed to high-ranking government jobs, some detractors charged her with nepotism. However, some of these issues were less related to her poor leadership than to persisting structural problems (Vito, 2000).

Low state operational and human resource capacities, widespread illiteracy, pervasive corruption in local political culture and the public sector, and deteriorating national infrastructure are a few of them (despite donor-funded improvements under Sirleaf). The Ebola outbreak hurt Liberia's potential for development and economic progress during Sirleaf's second term. Despite Sirleaf's conflicting internal opinions, the Liberians supported her, especially the female population. She also received praise from her fellow citizens for maintaining security. However, the UNMIL peacekeeping operation played a significant role in this outcome. Sirleaf was also praised on a global scale for her accomplishments in Liberia's socioeconomic development, post-war peacebuilding, and promotion of gender equality (Dwan et al., 2006). The United States awarded her the Presidential Medal of Freedom in 2007. President George W. Bush was one of the three recipients of the 2011 Nobel Peace Prize, and he respected her leadership and accomplishments. After resigning, she received the Mo Ibrahim Prize for exemplary governance in Africa in 2018. Some international observers, however, were critical of Sirleaf for supporting the prohibition of homosexuality in Liberia and the continuation of corruption under her rule (Tsimpo, 2010).

2.3.2. The 2017 Election

On October 10, 2017, Liberia conducted elections for the presidency and the House of Representatives. Twenty candidates were running for president, one of whom was a woman. The top contenders were Weah (CDC) and Vice President Joseph Boakai, who was in office then (Unity Party or UP). Senator Jewel Howard-Taylor of the National Patriotic Party (NPP), the organization of her ex-husband, the former president and convicted war criminal Charles Taylor, served as Weah's running partner for the CDC Coalition. Early in 2017, an uproar broke out in response to claims that UK prisoner Taylor had used cell phone talks to influence the creation of the CDC Coalition. They confirmed talking to Taylor on a supporter's phone during a party meeting but denied having private conversations with him. Later, he denied having connections to Taylor or any alleged Taylor agenda.

A total of 1.64 million people (or 75% of the electorate) cast ballots in the elections held in October. No, the candidate obtained the required 50% of the vote to win outright, forcing a runoff between the top two vote-getters, Boakai and Weah. We won this second competition, earning 61.5% of the vote. Weah's CDC won 21 of the 73 House seats, Boakai's UP won 19, and Independents won 12 seats. Ten minor parties competed for the remaining seats; they succeeded in winning at most five. The first-round third runner-up made severe charges that the first-round election had been tainted by fraud and irregularities, which were later joined by Boakai's UP and another party. This led to significant controversy before the presidential runoff, which took place on December 26, 2017 (Dwan et al., 2006).

They attempted to have the first-round vote thrown out through a National Election Commission (NEC) compliant and a Supreme Court lawsuit, but in vain. Concerns were raised about the possibility of a political crisis and potential instability due to their endeavor. Despite minor procedural irregularities, foreign and domestic election monitors rated the election as calm, transparent, well-conducted, and trustworthy. To conduct the election, the National Elections Commission (NEC) received significant funding from the United States and other nations (Tefft, 2005).

2.3.3. President Weah: New Administration

George Weah is a retired professional soccer player who achieved international fame for his sports accomplishments. His prior national political experience was confined to his time serving as a Senator beginning in 2014. In Liberia's Grand Kru County, he was born in 1966.

He was raised in poverty in a Monrovia slum and supposedly dropped out of school when he was young and finished high school. Although primarily of mixed Kru and Bassa ancestry, he has familial connections to counties dominated by other ethnic groups. He was criticized for his lack of formal schooling. Despite criticism during his failed 2005 presidential campaign, he received a high school diploma in 2007 and a bachelor's degree in business management in the United States (Riley, 1996).

He was elected to the Senate in 2014 to represent the Monrovia-area County of Montserrado. Better known to his admirers as King George, he is a former UNICEF Goodwill Ambassador and an aspiring singer. He has written songs promoting peace and raising awareness of the Ebola virus. His style is described as "warm, friendly, and giving." His rags-to-riches tale, Liberia's poverty philanthropy (such as funding a school in his old neighborhood and the national soccer team), and apparent empathy for him as a victim of social bias due to his lack of education all seem to have contributed to him gaining much support, particularly among the country's frequently impoverished and disenfranchised young population. Analysts questioned Weah's pick of Senator Jewel Howard-Taylor as his running partner because of potential links to her imprisoned former husband, Charles Taylor, and whether or not she was aware of the crimes committed during the war. However, Howard-Taylor and her supporters underlined the importance of voters evaluating her based on her qualifications and the quality of her record as an elected official. Howard-Taylor was chosen as a senator in 2005 and re-elected in 2014 after serving as the first lady. She has garnered national and local prominence in recent years for supporting initiatives to make homosexuality a crime that might result in the death penalty and to have Liberia legally recognized as a Christian country. She has several degrees from prestigious universities. She fought to secure improved public services and infrastructure delivery to her area while serving as a senator, where she supported many anti-corruption and transparency laws (Schroeder, 2006).

2.3.4. Economy

Significant economic difficulties are still present in Liberia. It is rumored that unemployment is high. Technical knowledge and training should be included, as well as cross-sectoral integration and value-added processing of commodities like lumber, rubber, and ores, even when detailed data are unavailable. National economic growth has been uneven and unnaturally inflated by assistance inflows. Consequently, the World Bank, the strength of Liberia's economic recovery following a decline in the cost of significant commodities shipments of raw materials and the ongoing consequences of the Ebola epidemic "will rely on the efficient economic diversification, creation of reliable institutions, and a streamlined political process.

Before the Ebola crisis, President Sirleaf's most significant accomplishments were economically speaking; even if extreme poverty continues to be pervasive, the nation faces several long-standing development issues. From $585 million in 2004, the first year following the second conflict, to well over $2 billion in recent years, the nominal Gross Domestic Product (GDP) increased steadily (2014-2017).

The real GDP growth then abruptly decreased, mainly due to the Ebola outbreak, according to the International Monetary Fund (IMF), from 8.8% in 2013, the year before the breakout hit, to 0.7% in 2014 and 0.01% in 2015. After that, it fell by 1.6% in 2016 before rebounding to 2.5% in 2017. Even though it had increased from $224 when Sirleaf entered office, GDP per capita, at $729 in 2017, is still low. Liberia's pre-epidemic prosperity depended partly on substantial inflows of development money predicated on donor faith in Sirleaf, on her government's negotiating several FDI deals with an emphasis on natural resources, and, to a lesser extent, on public investment in the agricultural sector.

According to reports, the Sirleaf government signed multi-year agreements with a combined potential value of $16 billion over 25 years. However, the existing FDI stocks represent less than half of this amount. With an emphasis on iron ore and gold mining, agriculture, forestry, rubber, and palm oil, FDI has concentrated on concession agreements. Additionally, there have been specific oil finds that may only be progressively developed depending on the state of the market. A significant recent dispute surrounding the distribution of rights to these sectors on allegations of corruption in distributing an offshore oil block that the American company Exxon later bought (Rob, 1999).

According to the US State Department, a "weak regulatory environment, corruption, lack of transparency, insufficient physical infrastructure, and limited private sector capabilities" hampered investment. According to the World Bank's 2018 Ease of Doing Business report, Liberia placed 172nd out of 190 nations. In addition to the assistance that has been so important in the reconstruction of crucial infrastructure and social services following the war, particularly in education and health, Liberia also received approximately $4.6 billion in international debt forgiveness in 2010 due to lengthy negotiations. Additionally, international financial institutions gave the Sirleaf administration high grades for its economic policy success (IFIs). As a result, Liberia gets significant IFI loans, grants, policy advice, and UN support in addition to the IFI loans, grants, advice, and technical agency help that it needs. The World Bank was funding fourteen projects in Liberia totaling about $598 million as of late 2017, in addition to helping provide regional bank programs. Although Liberia still has many unmet infrastructure requirements, building roads, water systems, and electrical infrastructure has been a critical focus of incremental progress. A significant focus of government development strategy in recent years, agriculture contributed around 36% of GDP in 2017 and is a crucial driver of non-extractive output, livelihoods, and microenterprise activity. The present administration will likely promote agricultural development, a key target of considerable support under the Feed the Future global food security project like the Sirleaf administration did (Remy, 1995).

2.4. Human Rights, Security, and Governance Issues

The most recent annual human rights report from the State Department, which covered 2017, stated that the most severe issues concerning human rights included "extrajudicial killings by police; police abuse, harassment, and intimidation of detainees and others; arbitrary arrest and detention; extreme rape, domestic abuse, female genital mutilation/cutting (FGM/C), criminalizing same-sex sexual behavior, and trafficking in persons are examples of violence against women and children that are often accompanied by press harassment, official corruption, and a lack of accountability (Johnson, 2004).

Impunity from justice for those who committed atrocities during the civil wars and those responsible for ongoing and current crimes was another fundamentally important issue. However, intermittent and ineffective government attempts to look into and bring charges against those accused of recent abuses, whether in the security forces or elsewhere in the government. The report also observed that public faith in government institutions was undermined by corruption at all levels of government (Dwan & Laura, 2006).

Many of these conclusions have been mirrored in U.N. reports on Liberia. The country is impacted by a "high incidence of sexual and gender-based violence; harmful traditional practices, such as female genital mutilation [FGM], forcible initiation into secret societies, trial by ordeal and accusations of witchcraft; curtailment of the freedom of speech; and limited national capacity and resources to promote and protect human rights," according to a mid-2017 report on UNMIL operations and general developments. Despite post-war advancements, similar earlier assessments have revealed flaws in the institutions and sectors of law enforcement. President Sirleaf issued an executive decree temporarily outlawing FGM before she left office (for a year). Observers have occasionally expressed worries about press limitations, mainly because of libel lawsuits where people or governmental authorities have demanded significant damages awards in cases frequently brought on seemingly questionable legal bases.

Liberia is included as a Tier Watch List nation under the Trafficking Victims Protection Act in the 2017 U.S. State Department Trafficking in Persons (TIP) Report (TVPA, Division A of P.L. 106-386, as amended, and its reauthorizations). This implies that Liberia did not show more extraordinary efforts compared to 2016, when it was a Tier nation, even though it is trying to comply with basic U.S. requirements for ending trafficking (i.e., one that did not meet such standards but was attempting to meet them). According to the research, Liberia "is both a source and a destination country for men, women, and children forced into domestic slavery, begging, sex trafficking, labor in the street, alluvial diamond mines, and rubber plantations. The research also claims that although there is some international trafficking, such victimization primarily happens in Liberia (Nicolas, 1997).

2.4.1. Good Governance

All facets of a nation's government are included under "governance." There are various traits of good governance. It adheres to the rule of law and is democratic, consensus-based, responsible, open, and responsive. In general, effective management calls for fair legal frameworks that are imposed impartially by an independent judiciary; its judgments and application are transparent or adhere to pre-established laws and regulations. Accountability is essential to effective governance since it can only be accomplished with openness and the rule of law. The public and stakeholders must keep governmental institutions, the commercial sector, and civil society groups responsible (Outran, 1990). A representative democracy with full involvement is also necessary for good governance. A key component of effective government is political engagement in legislative processes.

2.5. Institutions and Good Governance

In his most recent book, Douglass North, the Nobel laureate who wrote Understanding the Process of Economic Change, reaffirms that excellent institutions breed effective governance. Because they supply the fundamental factors that determine economic performance and the incentive structure of a society, institutions are essential in the long and short terms. Economic behavior is governed by official institutions (constitutions, laws, and regulations) and informal (social norms, practices, and traditions) principles. Institutions explicitly provide the framework of rules and incentives that influence how individuals, groups, and businesses use resources while making political and economic decisions or how they "play the game." North (2004) asserts that economic expansion and activity occur when rewards motivate people to produce. However, economies stagnate when they support exploitative or unproductive activity. Traditional civilizations may be able to meet their demands through informal human interactions and social networks. At the same time, contemporary economies— require established political, judicial, and economic laws because of their specialization and intricate division of labor. Political and financial organizations establish the circumstances necessary for the operation of a modern economy by establishing specific game rules. In 2006, formal institutions promoted rising production by guaranteeing property rights, building a legislature and judicial system, and enacting adaptable legal frameworks that permitted various organizational forms.

According to North, institutions "enhance growth" through lowering transaction costs and uncertainty. As a result, North's paradigm is frequently referred to as "new institutionalism" because its fundamental concepts are derived from an analysis of "transaction costs" — costs associated with the imperfection of real-world institutions that must be overcome in economic activity to take place. The institutional framework explicitly impacts growth because it is essential to the amount spent on transactions and transformations that are coherent with the production process. When property rights of the rule of law are lacking and not enforced, transaction costs are significantly greater (Alexis, 1961).

In these circumstances, private companies often work on a small scale and rely on extralegal methods. The parties know that an item or service will be supplied when it is paid for, which encourages exchange and commerce. In contrast, an institutional system that offers impartial third-party enforcement of agreements discourages it. According to North (2001), effective institutions can reduce transaction costs or expenses spent while conducting an economic trade because institutions and the enforcement of norms play a significant role in determining the costs of dealing. Transaction costs must be reduced via political and financial institutions to adequately increase the number of trade profits that may be realized. Despite the abundance of institutional regulations, North (and others) concur that safeguarding private property rights is essential to economic success. Because contemporary economies depend on property rights and efficient, impersonal contract enforcement, these factors are critical to lowering market uncertainty.

Conversely, social bonds, voluntary restrictions, and exclusion are less effective in a big, complicated, and impersonal economy. According to North, each market is unique and needs a specific combination of official and informal norms and the necessary enforcement methods to function effectively (Philip, 2014).

Furthermore, crucial factors like technology, information prices, and political regimes may change over time and increase transaction costs; something other than what makes a market function successfully in one era may not be acceptable in another. As a result, economic performance is mainly dependent on "adaptive efficiency," or the political system's success in establishing institutions that are fruitful, stable, fair, widely accepted, and flexible enough to be changed or replaced in response to political and economic feedback. This is because the kind and quality of institutions that support markets only account for a small portion of what determines financial performance (Patrick, 2001). This also holds for taking part in politics. When the National Legislature's legislative process depends on openness, accountability, and participation, it must support economic growth. The voters should be encouraged to participate in the political process by offering their opinions on the promulgation, creation, assessment, implementation, and change of public policies that will impact their daily lives.

2.5.1 Democracy and Economic Development

Under theocratic leadership, political institutions like the National Legislature are functional and essential for economic growth. Democracies can best maintain adaptive efficiency because democracy and institution development work hand in hand to foster effective governance and economic prosperity. It is no coincidence that all stable democracies have high economic growth rates and political engagement over generations. A stable democracy is strongly correlated with economic development, which is one of the most conclusive results of about two decades of research on democratization, though, as Chong argues, there is some evidence of a "political Kuznets curve" in which democracy has an immediate tendency to increase inequality while having a long-term trend to reduce it (Robert, 2009).

Today, liberal democracy is recognized as the best form of governance and deservedly has almost universal favor (Goodlad, 2004). According to the "procedural minimum," liberal democracy is a system of government in which voters are given the authority to elect and remove leaders through transparent institutional frameworks in a contest for the public's support. A genuinely representative democratic government, in the opinion of Robert Dahl, dean of democratic studies, must be founded on the principles of popular sovereignty, competitive political participation, and representation, an independent judiciary, free, fair, and regular elections, universal suffrage, freedom of expression, freedom of conscience, the unrestricted right to form political associations and take part in political life, inclusive citizenship, and adherence to the co (Okolo, 1989).

For a long time, academics have argued that democracies have inherent institutional advantages that foster economic growth. According to Nobel laureate Sen (2016), democracies boost the welfare of people with low incomes compared to other political systems and enrich human lives by offering political and civil rights. Second, they provide leaders with political incentives to meet the wants and desires of the populace. That is, democracies are perceived as being receptive to the demands and pressures of the public because the right to rule derives from popular support expressed in competitive elections, or as Robert Dahl noted in the past, governmental responsiveness to citizens' demands is built into periodically held electoral contests protected by legally recognized individual rights. This is supported by several research. For instance, the American Journal of Political Science (2005) found convincing evidence that democracy contributed to increased educational spending in examining 44 African governments. Similarly, Aveeno, Brown, and Hunter discovered a strong correlation between democracy and increased spending on social services, health care, and education (Marton, 2005).

Third, equality and justice may depend on the free discourse and discussion that characterize open democracies. This is known as the "constructive function" of democracy. Amartya Sen points out that this explains, for instance, the astounding fact that, in the horrible history of famines worldwide (Moore, 2009). The people's political involvement in the decision-making process is called democracy. The participation of the populace in the legislative process is crucial to this argument.

2.5.2. Democracy and Good Governance

A common misconception among observers is that establishing a democratic regime would also quickly consolidate democratic institutions and practices. However, cross-national country experiences reveal that the authority of an old government, which is constrained by its own administrative and bureaucratic culture and traditions, may be astonishingly resistant to change. Furthermore, the idea that democracy inevitably entails a break with the past raises the possibility that authoritarianism, elitism, and social exclusion may coexist with a nominal democratic regime. Because democracies may grow yet remain fragmentary, degrade, or collapse, democratic consolidation may be protracted and complex. According to O'Donnell and Schmitt's original study, the level of democracy can be significantly determined by the transition pattern (Kangou, 2005).

The most fruitful are "pasted transitions" between moderates in civil society and "soft-liners" in the previous government. However, one side will set the rules when it is stronger than the other. An autocratic transition pattern will result if the powerful are autocrats, which is frequently the case. An unstable government is most frequently the result of power being distributed more evenly between "autocrats" and "reformers." Nearly 25 years after the third wave of democratization, most places continue to have flawed democracies. Zakaria's pessimistic view that "liberty is not nourishing, whereas democracy is" tends to be confirmed by the realities on the ground. Why does this paradox exist, and how can it be resolved? Similar to what Diamond and O'Donnell previously referred to as "hybrid regimes," when authoritarian tactics are combined with democratic democracies, O'Donnell once dubbed "declarative democracy," Zakaria points out that although the concept of democracy (in the sense of giving power to the people) has gained popularity quickly, it is less obvious how far these ideas are being institutionalized and used again in the political system (Douglas, 2008).

In most circumstances, however, the outcome is frequently the creation of what Zakaria refers to as "illiberal democracies"—a government that purposefully mixes the language of liberal democracy with illiberal rule. For instance, despite the nation's frequent, fiercely contested, multiparty elections, which classify it as an "electoral" democracy, the state's routine operations are characterized by arbitrariness and abuses. Similarly, political liberties and civil rights may be theoretically acknowledged but seldom upheld in practice; although formally considered independent, the court is readily overthrown, and the free press is frequently persecuted. According to Zakaria, the process of democratization has involved "opening up its politics to a much wider group of people who were previously marginalized" and "creating new political parties" that have made India "more democratic" but "less liberal." This is true even of well-established democracies like India.

As a result, illiberal democracy (i.e., a nominally democratic government devoid of constitutional liberalism and institutional checks) is not only potentially dangerous because it can lead to the erosion of freedom, the abuse of power, racial tensions, and conflict, but it also "has not proven to be an effective path to liberal democracy." Provocatively asserting that promoting constitutional liberty before promoting democracy is the best approach to transforming emerging or traditional cultures into liberal democracies, Zakaria makes a bold claim. This is due to the likelihood that electoral democracy will become authoritarian if formed before a group has obtained constitutional rights. According to Zakaria, democracy undermines liberty by trampling on freedom (Kathleen, 2005).

As an analogy, he makes the case that if free elections were held in Islamic nations, the majority of fundamentalist parties would win and then go on to obliterate liberty because "it would be one man, one vote, one time." According to Zakaria, "liberal authoritarian regimes" such as those in Singapore and earlier in South Korea, Taiwan, and Chile are best equipped to provide the constitutional liberal foundation from which democracy can finally emerge. It is undoubtedly unpersuasive to characterize authoritarian regimes that formerly controlled Taiwan, South Korea, or Chile as "liberal" or to generalize challenging nation experiences. Authoritarian governments that once ruled Taiwan, South Korea, or Chile are certainly not liberal. It appears that, rather than being driven by their inherent liberalism, these authoritarian governments were pushed by the demands of civil society toward greater political openness and, finally, democracy (Jonathan, 2002).

The PRC situation also demonstrates that a one-party government does not necessarily foster democratic principles, as was previously argued. The "sequencing fallacy," as Carothers incisively notes, "rests on the incorrect two-part premise that those nations democratizing are intrinsically ill-suited for these responsibilities and that a considerable proportion of autocrats can and will function as generators of rule-of-law development and state builders." Despite the plausibility of Zakaria's reasoning, his recommendations are not (John, 1991).

2.5.3. Democratic Nation and State Building

The distinction between de jure and de facto states was made by Robert Jackson twenty years ago. Many de jure states, however, are quasi-states since they are recognized as legal sovereign entities by other countries even though they lack many characteristics of a functional government. The labels "weak," "failed," "collapsing," "fragile," "rogue," or "post-conflict states" are frequently used to refer to these quasi-states in the modern era. Regardless of the title, these governments provide complex issues for democratic administration, economic growth, and global stability. They cannot offer necessary public goods like security, law, order, education, and other crucial services or set up sound legal regulations. Some estimates place the number of weak nations at approximately fifty, whereas the World Bank has recognized about thirty low-income countries as being "under stress."

The issue is making the "state" an effective and accountable sovereign in an environment of lawlessness, violence, and impunity when the "state" lacks even those essential characteristics of sovereignty. However, how can this be done? Democracies cannot thrive in anarchic environments, as countless examples of failed democratization demonstrate. Nothing is, in the words of Rotberg, "as vital as the supply of security, especially human security," amid a "hierarchy of political commodities." The development of a government with a monopoly of legitimate authority and the ability to enforce laws over the whole state's territory is at the heart of state-building, according to Fukuyama, who supports the "staleness first" position (Francis, 2004).

So, it is crucial to provide political stability and security. Once an order is confirmed, it is essential to simultaneously strengthen the emerging institutions of governance and the rule of law, as well as the growth of formal representative organizations like political parties—which serve as a vital conduit between the general public and the bodies charged with deciding on legal policy. To provide essential services like public security, law and order, and convict management, it may also be necessary for some contexts for the legal state structures to form alliances with a variety of local nonstarter intermediaries and competing sources of authority; however, these arrangements should only be used as a temporary measure before the formal governing bodies are consolidated (Gockowski, 2010).

Furthermore, it is crucial to stress that creating a democratic state is not cheap. State-building will require external finance and logistical assistance—sometimes for lengthy periods—because weak and failing nations cannot generate cash independently. This implies that the whole world community, especially the wealthy countries, must be prepared to continue on the current track. However, this does not mean that grandiose and excessively ambitious schemes for nation-building are the solution, as Carothers and others have suggested (Brancait, 2006).

Building a country or state is not a technical activity; instead, the goals should be precisely focused, the expectations should be maintained reasonably, and so on. Every civilization will instead create institutions specific to its history, culture, customs, and ethnic make-up. So, it is crucial to adjust to the local ways of life. Fukuyama's warning to democratic nation-builders that there is a distinction between "state" and "country" creation is also something to bear in mind. A country is more than just a state; it has everyday experiences, culture, values, language, and a feeling of identity. If a condition is a government, then a nation is much more than that.

In comparison to state-building, nation-building is far more ambitious and complex. In contrast to what Fukuyama observes, persuading individuals divided by area, religion, or ethnicity to live in the same community and have similar interests is much more complicated. Establishing an army or a police force is straightforward. As a result, establishing a democratic state and country involves two distinct steps (Brooks, Douglas) (2008). To construct a state, political engagement is crucial. Since it is viewed as such by the populace, the legislative arm of government is the first branch of the federal government. The people must be informed and actively determine which laws should be established to serve their interests, as their voices are being represented.

At the very least, it must involve the development or reinforcement of fundamental governmental institutions, such as the security apparatus, the judicial system, the economic organizations, and the social welfare systems, including the education and healthcare systems. According to Fukuyama's argument, the first phase should focus on restoring basic infrastructure, creating law and order, and kicking off the economy to stabilize the nation. After stability is reached, the second phase must start. This should involve establishing autonomous political and economic institutions that will eventually allow for the democratic rule of law and economic expansion. The fact that the alternatives are worse is arguably the most vigorous defense for such cautious state expansion.

In addition to serving as a safeguard against extravagant, ultimately costly, and ineffective experiments like those in Iraq, it also implies that leaving unstable governments to their own devices might lead to the resurgence of civil wars and interstate inmates, making the long-term costs far greater (Brooks &Douglas, 2008).

Last but not least, involvement is necessary for the governance process. Effective governance is a problem for many nations that are operating. Building state capacity is needed to halt this trend, solidify just power, and establish the rule of law. "Democracy is a type of government of a state," remarked Linz and Stephan succinctly. Therefore, until a modern polity establishes itself as a state, it cannot consolidate democracy. The government institutions must be merit-based, ally-organized, and rule-based for the state to be considered adequately capable. This improves the state's capacity to provide public services, uphold some level of regulatory control, enforce laws, and uphold social order (Atul, 1986).

This is strikingly shown by the experience of the East Asian countries, which are only starting to industrialize. East Asia's "development states" were essential in driving economic expansion and reducing poverty significantly. Building effective democratic states requires bolstering the formal powers embodied in the executive and legislative branches, similar to the "top-down" authoritarian East Asian developmental states so that they can convert a variety of partisan preferences into practical policy options either through majority rule or formation of workable coalitions (Brooks, 2008, page number). This can only be done by involving the electorate in the legislative process and allowing for political engagement.

2.6. Corruption and Related Challenges to Trust in State Institutions

Along with development, economic progress, and public sector probity, corruption has long been a significant concern for Liberians. The State of Peace, a 2016 report by Catholic Relief Services and the Justice and Peace Commission (JPC), revealed widespread public anxiety about corruption and worries about the stability of the supposedly stable peace in Liberia. Widespread discontent with government performance was also discovered in the 2015 Afro barometer polls, particularly concerning infrastructure issues, economic management, education, unemployment, and farming (Anke, 2004).

The Catholic Relief Services/JPC report identified horizontal differences characterized by "regional, ethnic, religious, and political" and highlighted concerns over land and property issues. "Vertical" threats to social cohesiveness are caused by "crony capitalism, rent-seeking, and a weak civil society" and "urban vs. rural and young vs. old cleavages." Additionally, poverty and better "livelihoods, education, and jobs, especially for young people" are in "desperate need," as other critical difficulties. The Sirleaf administration made several attempts, with varying degrees of success, to increase governmental openness and fortify the rule of law. When Sirleaf departed office, corruption was widely believed to remain pervasive, despite the nation's ranking on Transparency International's Corruption Perceptions Index falling from 150th internationally in 2006 to 122nd in 2017. Instead of blaming a lack of political will, she said that her limited success in combating corruption was "the intractability of reliance and dishonesty bred through years of suffering and terrible government" (Egert, 2009, page number).

2.6.1. Legislature

Despite a U.S.-funded legislative strengthening initiative (2009–2013) and other donor help, the capability of the legislature is allegedly still inadequate. Election turnover and, occasionally, the selection of inexperienced candidates with little formal education are contributing causes. Additionally, some lawmakers have been charged with using their positions for personal benefit and have opposed efforts to impose stricter anti-corruption regulations. A history of executive branch domination, weak political party discipline, a lack of skilled civil society issue advocacy, a weak rule of law, corruption, and informal, frequently self-interested decision-making are institutional obstacles to the efficacy of legislation (Eleanor, 1990).

2.6.2. U.S. Assistance

Most of the post-war non-Ebola bilateral aid from the United States to Liberia has been managed by USAID and the State Department. A $25.7 million MCC Compact struck in late 2015 has increased this assistance since the beginning of 2016. In FY2016 and FY2017, the State Department and USAID provided $112 million in bilateral aid. The $29 million for FY2018 and $43 million for FY2019 budget proposals from the Trump administration. The State Department and approximately $618 million in emergency money granted by Congress were also given to USAID, encouraging the US Ebola response in Liberia, as was previously mentioned. In recent years, USAID's non-Ebola aid has concentrated on five often converging areas: economic growth, health, education, democracy, and governance, as well as cross-cutting concerns, including youth development, gender justice, and environmental preservation. Much of this assistance was given through global or African-specific presidential development projects, such as Power Africa, the Global Health Initiative, Feed the Future, and the President's Malaria Initiative, launched by President Bush and extended by President Obama. Liberia also participates in the U.S. Young African Leaders Initiative (YALI), which promotes the growth of upcoming young African leaders in business, civics, and public administration through an exchange-based fellowship program (David, 2005).

Aid that the department manages helped the legal system, including the police and courts, military education, capacity building, and, in collaboration with DOD, security sector reform targeting the armed forces. UN High Commission has also received funding from the State Department for the UNHCR's refugee initiatives, offering vital protection, aid with returning home, and service delivery to Ivoirian refugees in Liberia. Additionally, the US contributes to funding other UN entities that assist Liberia and has paid slightly over a quarter of all UN peacekeeping missions of the UNMIL's expenses (e.g., $106 million in FY2016 and a projected $62 million for FY2017).

The building of post-war democratic institutions with a particular focus on Elections and the development of legislative ability. Another tool for enhancing governance aimed to improve fiscal management and controls, transparency, accountability, and effectiveness of public administration, as well as public sector institutional reform and decentralization, service delivery, citizen participation in governance, tax collection, taxpayer accountability, and responsibility, support for legal professionals, and anti-corruption initiatives (Ceete, 2009).

2.6.3. Security Cooperation

With roughly $250 million in American help, the Armed Forces of Liberia (AFL), a force of around 2,100 people, was established. Additionally, this support helped appoint and screen new soldiers while disbanding the previous military. Following the AFL's operational status in 2010, US assistance changed from primarily contractor-based basic training and capacity-building to military-to-military mentorship under an advising program known as Operation Onward Liberty, which ended in August 2016. The modest Liberian Coast Guard was also established with American assistance. Regular interactions and engagement with US military personnel help ongoing efforts to improve the security sector. Regional Peacekeeping Operations (PKO) funding from the State Department has been used to support these initiatives. Using funds for Foreign Military Financing (FMF), the State Department has sponsored the AFL's training, supplies, and advising services. International Military Education and Training (IMET) is a program the State Department supports. Professionalization of senior and middle military and civilian defense employees emphasizes management abilities, civil-military interactions, and human rights (Arend, 1984).

The DOD Defense Institution Reform Initiative has assisted the Liberian Ministry of Defense to improve its capability. The AFL has received regular training from the DOD Defense Institute of International Legal Studies to strengthen its military justice skills. The Michigan U.S. National Guard State Partnership Program and U.S. Africa Command frequently collaborate with Liberia. The AFL dispatched 50 soldiers to Mali in 2013 as part of its first-ever foreign troop contribution to assist the MINUSMA U.N. peacekeeping effort there. This was the second significant AFL mission; the first was a deployment inside Liberia in 2012 to support enhancing border security with Côte d'Ivoire. The AFL also assisted Operation United Assistance, the American military's reaction to the Ebola virus, particularly with the engineering needed for Ebola treatment facilities. A teenager was killed by the AFL's use of live rounds, which drew protests from the US ambassador, among others. The AFL nevertheless assisted in enforcing the Ebola-related quarantine. Although AFL capacity has continuously increased, there have been instances of absenteeism, troop protests about housing conditions, and occasional indiscipline (Baldwin, 2011).

2.7. The Political Setting for the Conflict in Liberia

Exclusion politics and related economic policies of uneven opportunity implemented by the returned ex-slaves who formed the country have their roots in the early days of Liberia's struggle. The American Colonization Society (ACS) dropped out immigrants on the coasts of what would become Liberia in 1820–1822; they later organized themselves into a self-governing republic of three counties, Montserrado, Grand Bassa, and Sinoe, then left. Then, in 1847, they proclaimed themselves a sovereign, independent republic. In its preamble, the constitution established after independence made it plain who the settlers were: "We, the people of the Republic of Liberia, were originally the residents of the United States of North America." The term "Americo-Liberians" was appropriate, and the immigrants kept their distinct identity, which they eventually transformed into a reign of caprice and privilege over the natives. The Americo-Liberians increased their landmass by stealing land from the locals in the hinterland.

About 60 years after the country proclaimed independence, the hinterland residents, some of whose ancestors had been there as early as the 12th century, were "granted citizenship" to "unify" the nation. The political system was based on the one in the United States. However, its primary goal was to shield the repatriates from vague anxieties rather than promote a united country's growth. Native Americans were thus virtually kept out of politics for the first century. When 17 non-commissioned officers with Native American ancestry violently seized political control in April 1980, they were sure they intended to overthrow an oppressive colonial rule but unclear about what to replace it with. In actuality, they imposed their form of government without regard for institutional limitations, accelerating Liberia's downfall. Prison, however, had far deeper roots, and some would argue that the plunge into convict began much earlier and was only intensified by the events of April 1980. Early on, injustice was confronted with opposition. A prime example was the resistance to independence, or the time of freedom as a rejection of Montserrado County's unhealthful hegemony over the other counties. The Declaration of Independence came after a bitter Constitutional

Convention during which violence prevented eligible voters from casting their ballots in two of the three counties that make up the state (Vamvakidis, 1998).

All eligible voters in Sinoe County were barred from casting a ballot due to extensive violence, although only some voters in Grand Bassa County did so. The dominance of Montserrado County over the other counties, which sparked resistance to Liberia's independence, persists today and is reflected in the stark discrepancy between Montserrado, relatively prosperous, and the other fourteen poorer counties in Liberia. More accurately, wealthy metropolitan Monrovia continues to rule over extremely impoverished rural Liberia. The state's successive governing elites were never quite sure of their identity as either non-Africans or Africans chosen by Providence to redeem Africans. Indeed, "Christianizing" and "civilizing" the Indians were among the ACS's objectives. One outcome was that the repatriates, who had faced prejudice in North America and were seen as inferior to white people and the illegitimate light-skinned children of enslavers, constructed a virtual caste system in the new region. Until the 1870s, the culture developed into a settler democracy in which the native population was treated even lower than the darker-skinned repatriates and mulattoes who dominated society. Darker-skinned repatriates gained power in 1876 and have been a significant part of society's elite ever since. The elite acted like colonial lords, and as a result, they not only had no sympathy for the region or many locals but also detested both.

This oddity impacted policies governing resource allocation, growth, and service provision. This black colonialism somewhat explains the "deadly convicts" battles between the locals and the repatriates between 1822 and 2037 (Wincoop, 2004, page number).

2.7.1. African Democracy and Popular Power

The contemporary tendency in African pro-democracy social movement efforts against the authoritarian government, which is frequently justified but disguised as (pseudo) democracy, is critically examined in this article. It offers a critical evaluation of the power trends among the continent's populace and the chances for their pursuit of a fair and inclusive political system. Following a lengthy history of resistance against colonial domination, post-World War II nationalist conflicts and postcolonial fights against authoritarian single-party/military control culminated in the post-Cold War "third wave" of liberation movements.

In the 1990s, democracy overthrew many of Africa's autocratic regimes. The uprisings and demonstrations that took place in 2011 in Tunisia, Egypt, Uganda,

Malawi, Swaziland, Senegal, and Botswana are just the latest in a long line of popular African resistance movements against oppressive regimes and unpopular laws that date back to the anti-colonial struggles of the 1940s and 1950s. The end of formal colonialism did not end the struggle for justice and freedom (Wilcox, 2010).

The core tenets of the nationalist project, democracy, inclusive development, nation-building, and national unity, which had been well recorded throughout the last 50 years of Africa's independence, have vanished from the political agenda of post-independent African governments. The gap between the elite-controlled state and African society grew significantly by the halfway point of the continent's second decade of independence. At the same time, resentment simmered under the surface. Mass discontent was partly fueled by the disintegration of the nationalist coalition between the elite and the peasants, the transition to military/single-party control, and the stifling of alternative voices and dissent in the name of national unity and growth. Though intended to be accessible and uplifting, the so-called "nationalist development project" instead served as a vehicle for those in positions of authority to enrich themselves and their political allies while leaving most of their populations to fend for themselves (Anderson, 2004).

The ruling class needed to have supported economic growth in rural regions, where most people reside, or to deliver basic amenities to the expanding urban population. However, due to the 1980s financial crisis, widespread discontent with authoritarian governments erupted throughout sub-Saharan Africa. People started calling for radical political and economic changes and adopting multiparty democratic political systems. "Africa's second independence" came to be known due to these mass upheavals. They first offered the most positive proof of the development of the new institutions and principles that must serve as the foundation for a significant democratic effort. Similar to how the current upheavals in North Africa have sparked popular movements throughout the Arab world, the mass mobilizations in sub-Saharan Africa in the late 1980s and early 1990s coincided with the fall of communism in Eastern Europe. As internal pressures in Africa intensified, sometimes made worse by the deteriorating economic conditions, African tyrants could no longer rely on Washington or Moscow to save them with the end of East-West competition. With their backs against the wall, these authoritarian leaders started to open the political process, albeit grudgingly. This resulted in many parties, but still needed a handover of power to the populace. Liberia was one of Africa's 54 civilian or military dictatorships in 1990; there were only five exceptions (Stohl, 2005).

2.7.2. Barriers to effective governance: External Requirements

The next portion of this study will discuss the most critical issues in Liberia regarding implementing sound governance principles. However, the fact that donors frequently impose good governance is a general issue with implementing it. This may compel uncooperative leaders to adhere to particular best practices but impedes ownership of such policies and procedures. As a result, dedication can be restricted. The issue will worsen when precise definitions of good governance differ or conflict.

However, it must be acknowledged that the absence of ownership or external forces cannot be an excuse for rejecting—the idea of appropriate best practices or good governance. A cautious approach is required, adjusting to local situations and customs and establishing a genuine collaboration between nations and donors. However, the truth remains that many people are self-interested in having excellent administration. This is accepted by the AU's stated goals above and even the Liberian Constitution. The General Principles of National Policy in Chapter II of the Constitution of Liberia read like a checklist of Good Governance aims and activities, even if the phrase is not defined and is used to convey verbs (Wallace, 1972). "We the people" is the overarching idea or tenet.

2.7.3. Democracy and Human Rights

Despite opposition charges of electoral fraud, the most recent free and fair elections were held in Liberia in October and November 2005; despite opposition claims of electoral fraud, this is a significant step toward the democratization of Liberia. However, according to the International Crisis Group (ICG), they must constitute more essential and sufficient circumstances. Respect for fundamental human rights, such as freedom of expression, the right to assemble, and the rights of minorities, is another aspect of democracy. Liberia still has a long way to go, given the hostility toward the Mandingo minority, pervasive oppression of women, and occasionally threatening to kill journalists. Individual governance analyses also reveal this.

Furthermore, to prevent the misuse of power, real democracies must regulate the executive branch effectively. Presidency-based governance systems, like those in Liberia, run the danger of becoming autocratic and less responsive and responsible. The domestication of the executive in Liberia will be primarily made possible by civil society, the legislature, and the judiciary (Barkey, 1967). The legislative arm of government is the critical institution that can enforce a viable democracy through political responsibility and participation. To do this, elected officials must uphold these values to prevent the nation's dark past of societal disorganization, which stalked the country for 15 years and left consequences on Liberia's public administration. It is essential to promote citizen engagement in legislative decision-making.

CHAPTER THREE.
RESEARCH METHODOLOGY

3.1. Introduction

This chapter outlines the research methods used in the study's design, population, sample size and sampling strategies, research tools, data gathering processes, and data processing techniques.

3.2. Research Method

The study employed the qualitative research method in that it sought to inquire about the involvement of the people in political governance -A Liberian Dilemma: A Case Study of the National Legislature.

People research to learn new information methodically and broaden their knowledge. It is essential to notice that this definition includes the terms "systematic approach" and "to find out stuff," which are both crucial. Research is said to be "systematic" if it is based on logical relationships rather than merely beliefs (Saunders & Thornhill, 2009). It accurately captures the study project's primary notion (William, 2001). "To find out stuff" might have a variety of meanings or applications for your research. These could involve outlining, clarifying, comprehending, critiquing, and analyzing.

3.3. Research Design

Experimental research methods were employed in this investigation (Darlington, 2014). The preliminary study of a fictitious or theoretical concept is known as empirical research. In this scenario, a researcher has an idea or has noticed something and wants to learn more about it. An exploratory research study looks to build the framework for more research or see if an existing theory can explain the observations. Most of the time, experimental research builds the foundation for subsequent studies.

According to Neumann (2006), a theory's predetermined ideas, constructions, and hypotheses are the basis for the deductive process. Linkages are outlined using testable hypotheses to support the theory, and efforts are made to gather more specific empirical data. The inductive method begins with collecting data and formulating perspectives using the facts obtained (Saunders, 2007). A qualitative and deductive approach was the most appropriate for the study because the researcher's goal was clearly stated, it was intended to sample a sizable number of cases, and it would be used to test hypotheses on the factors that influenced political participation in Liberian elections and decision-making.

3.4. Population of the Study

The entire group of units for which survey data were utilized to conclude is considered the target population for a survey, according to Brenda (2014). The target population defines which survey results are supposed to be generalized. The first step in creating a study is defining the research goals. The second stage ought to be representing the target population. Brenda (2014) also pointed out that the target populations must be specified clearly since this will impact whether the sampled cases are accepted or rejected for the survey. It is necessary to define the target population's geographic and temporal features. The people of this study consisted of members of the National Legislature of both Houses, totaling 102 Legislators in best practices of Good Governance about people to Political Governance. Therefore, the population of this study was 102 Legislators. According to Ary (2002), for a researcher to gather the needed data for a survey of either a social, educational, economic, or scientific nature, the inclusion of every element of the population of the analysis becomes necessary.

3.5. Sample Size and Sampling Techniques

Respondents from both Houses of the National Legislature are sampled for the study using the purposive sampling methodology. The researcher decides which units to include in the sample based on their willingness and ability to participate in the survey or their familiarity with the research topic. This is known as purposeful sampling, a type of non-random sampling. As a result, the researcher purposefully chose two House of Representative representatives and three (3) senators. The reasons for these selections were firstly based on the availability and willingness of the participants. Also, the period of their services in the Legislature in either of the two houses (Senate and Representatives) was crucial to the election criteria. Also, the researcher was very concerned about gender representation in the participants in the selection process but relied on who was willing to participate and available. Usually, these decisions are made based on experiences and knowledge. Burns & Grove (2010) state that the researcher chose the units to be sampled based on their expertise, the productivity of the sample to address the research questions, and the review period used by this study, which was from 2006 to 2012.

3.6. Research Instruments

The Instrument used by the researcher was open-ended interview questions. The data of this study was collected through face-to-face interviews with five respondent-legislators.

Twumasi (2000) acknowledged that selecting a particular method to collect data must be social science research. Further, the researcher kept in mind the type of people they were dealing with, the nature of the social situation, the mood of the social environment, and the psychology of the people.

3.7. Data Collection Procedures

Data Collection Procedures was hinged on a letter of introduction from the Director of the MBA/MPA to the individual members of the National Legislature at the Capitol Building who were the respondents; the letter also introduced the research topic. Data collection is systematically gathering and measuring information on variables of interest that enables one to answer stated research questions and evaluate outcomes (Kabir, 2016). The researcher also visited the research site (Capitol Building) many times during the research. Due to their busy schedules, the researcher met with the participants numerous times. The researcher explained the study's objectives to the 5 participants. After their consent, a face-to-face interview, some through telephone and video calls, was held for several days intermittently to collect the needed data. The open-ended questions asked during the interview were intended to get the participants' perspectives, such as: What is the relationship between lawmakers and their constituents? How are the electorates fully participating in legislative activities? What are the challenges electorates face with their lawmakers? The researchers were cooperative with this study as most of this is the first of its kind since they have been in the Legislature. Some of the respondents agree to respond to the questionnaire on the telephone.

3.8. Data Analysis Procedures

The data collected for this study were recorded, coded, and constructed (grouped) into tables based on the biographical data collected from the 5 National Legislature, the First Government branch participants. The researcher developed open-ended interview questions' responses into themes and sub-themes. This biographical information, such as gender, educational status, marital status, and county of origin, formed the basis of the data categorization presented in tables and subsequent analyses. Once all preliminary procedures were addressed, the researcher conducted the interview and transcribed each interview from audio recordings into themes and subthemes. To achieve this data analysis process, it requires the recording of the conversations. After the recording process was done, the transcripts were done and recorded in a spreadsheet Microsoft program on the computer. The transcripts were analyzed, and codes were identified. From the coding, the data was analyzed into concepts, themes, and patterns. From these laborious steps and processes, findings and analysis were made on the data collected from the participants, which inform the research.

3.9. Ethical Consideration

Ethics can affect many research-based decisions (Burkholder, et al., 2020, p.199). Burkholder et al. (2020) list ethical issues as participant recruiting, instrumentation, data storage, analysis, and dissemination (p. 161). The researcher obtained permission from the University of Liberia Graduate School and the participants. To protect participants, the researcher described the study's goals and avoided bias. Volunteering information may make participants distrustful and apprehensive. Participants can disengage whenever needed during the study. These were advice given to participants by the researcher. The researcher followed all ethical guidelines to obtain informed consent. Thus, the research participants were informed of the benefits, importance, and consequences of participant data. Before consenting to the study, participants were given enough information to make informed decisions while confidentiality was emphasized by the researcher to the participants.

CHAPTER FOUR.

DATA PRESENTATION, INTERPRETATION, DISCUSSION, AND ANALYSIS

4.1. Introduction

This chapter presents data gathered, reviews the results and analysis of the qualitative data, and then compiles the Interviewed open-ended questions about the lives and effects of the findings. The findings were also comprehensively discussed, given previous research findings and available literature, where applicable, to identify similarities and dissimilarities between this study and prior studies and literature. The last chapter three gave a comprehensive description of the research methodology.

4.2. Data Presentation and Interpretation

For the data presentation and interpretation processes, the researcher focused on the data gathered from 5 (five) respondents who are two members of the lower house (Representatives) and three members are the upper house (Senate in the research through the research instruments (open-ended interview questions).

4.2.1. Demographic Profile of the Respondents

Table 1: Gender of Respondent

Sex	Number	Percentage
Male	3	60
Female	2	40

Table 1: Gender of Respondents Source: field data 2020

According to table one, the respondents' gender was three male, which represents sixty percent, and two females, which represents forty percent. This means there were more male respondents in this research than female respondents. This representation of the sex or gender of the participants also helps show pictures about participation in political governance and the number of sex and gender in leadership. The records and data show that women are less in the Legislature as compared to their male counterparts. This is the rationale for this table demographic on sex and gender.

Table 2: Age Range of Respondents

Age	Number	Percentage
18-25	0	0
26-35	0	0
36-45	1	20
46-Above	4	80

Table 2: Age Range of Respondents Field data 2020

Table two, which is the age range of Legislator-Respondents, from 18-25, there was none found in this category; from 26-35, none was found in this category; from 36-45, one Legislator-Respondent constitutes 20%, 46 years above which is four Legislator-Respondents represents 80%. This means that four of the legislator-respondents were older. This table shows that persons of particular ages were not present in the Legislature at the time of the interview. The purpose of this demographic to should the level of representation and which age is dominant in the Legislature.

Table 3: Educational Level of Respondents

Education	Number	Percentage
College level	0	0
Bachelor's Degree Holder	3	60
Master's Degree Holder	2	40
Doctoral Degree Holder	0	0

Table 3: Educational Level of Respondents Field Data 2020

Table three shows the educational level of the Legislator-Respondents; none were college students; three were bachelor's degree holders who constituted sixty percent; none were master's students, and two were master's degree holders, who constituted forty percent. This demonstration aims to understand and know the level of education members of the Legislature have. While it is true that education is not a legal requirement to be a member of the Legislature, it is also essential to know the level of education that a member of the Legislature has in these contemporary times of national and international existence representing a particular constituency in the first branch of government.

Table 4: Respondents Group by Rank/Level

Rank	Number	Percentage
Senator	3	60
Representative	2	40

Table 4: Respondents Group by Rank/Level Field Data 2020

According to table four, of the respondents grouped by rank/level, three were senators represented sixty percent, and two representatives represented forty percent. This means that both houses of the national legislature were equally represented in this study. In the Liberian setting, when the Legislature is mentioned, it comprises the House of Representatives which is the lower house and the House of Senate which is referred to as a Upper House or the House of Elders. Ranking the Legislatures at this demographic demonstration is to show that not one segment of the Legislature was represented as a participant in the study. It included both the House of Representatives and House of Senate to get a broader perspective of the phenomenon under study - political participation at the Legislative level of government.

Table 5: Respondents' Length of Time in the Legislature

Length	Number	Percentage
0-6 yrs.	1	20
7-12 yrs.	4	80
Total	5	100

Table 5 Respondents' Length of Time in the Legislature Field data 2020

According to table five, of the five Legislator-Respondents interviewed, one Legislator-Respondent has served from 0 to six years, which is twenty percent. In comparison, four Legislator-Respondents have benefited from 7 to 12 years, which constitutes eighty percent. This indicates that most of the Legislator-Respondents have been in the National Legislature for a relatively extended time. Showing this gives the reader the perspective that these were participants will well inform knowledge of the workings of the Legislature and their perspectives provided indebt knowledge of what they are doing. Responses from these participants are rich.

4.3. Interview Questions with 5 Respondents from Both Houses of National Legislature

The researcher interviewed five respondents at the National Legislature on the topic under study. The face-to-face interview was conducted for several days, from September 12-30, 2020, with the 5 Legislators of the National Legislature at the Capitol Building, meaning at a separate time during this period.

4.3.1. What does the Electorate expect of their Lawmaker?

Respondent *–legislator one* said no, but based on their level of understanding, they only call town hall meetings to put before them except where a Legislator is interested in a piece of legislation, that is the only time they mobilize for their constituents to assemble in a town hall for discussion and after that everyone return to status quo. According to respondent-Senator two, in all engagements, no one asks any related questions on expectations from the lawmakers. He further stated that they only ask for executive funds. They are more interested in the county development funds used for development.

4.3.2. What is the electorate's participation or involvement in passing bills at the National Legislature?

Respondent *Senator two* answered that the people were not involved. There are no public hearings as the lawmakers only deliberate among themselves. In furtherance of this, they argue that the awareness should be done by the executive branch and not the legislature. According to Respondent five, about 40% of the respondents are aware, while 60% of the electorates are not aware. He further stated that only the educated electorates know about the passage of the Bill while the uneducated don't know anything about it. According to the respondent-*legislator*, people are sometimes unaware of some activities they initiate. According to Respondent *–Senator three*, Liberia has representative democracy; logically, the electorates are directly involved because of their representatives. Respondent-legislator categorically said that she had tried her best to engage her constituents in the process most of the time, but it's. Still, it's challenging as some electorates don't have time for this interactive legislative activity.

4.3.3. How is the record-keeping process at the National Legislature recording minutes of deliberations on the passage of bills for future reference?

Ans.: respondent two said Yes, the clerk of both houses keeps the minutes of the proceedings manually. Sometimes when deliberation is going on, the clerk of the

House is asked to do the recording. According to Respondent *Senator- three*, about 40% of the electorates attend while 60% don't listen. Given the new areas of radios, they feel inferior to getting involved. In addition, Respondent-*legislator one* said that the record-keeping at the Legislature is done manually, sometimes on a typewriter. Respondent-*legislator one* emphasized that she had raised her voice for digital storage of all legislative minutes, correspondences, and documents, but it is yet to happen. Still, the issue is either the low capacity of staff and personnel or no funding for purchasing technology machinery.

4.3.4. How the Citizens Engagement with the Legislators during legislative recess in their various constituencies to know and understand the legislative working of the Legislature?

Ans: According to **Respondent-***Senator three*, it is left with the description of the legislator, but under normal circumstances by right, these meetings should be called to inform the citizens to report to their constituents about happenings in their work in the Legislature. According to Respondent Senator-Three, most of their constituent's members don't bother them much. Respondent-legislator three said some legislators call for such meetings only when they are interested in a particular issue at the legislature; they do that because they want a political goal from that constituency. Respondent- *Senator one* said their constituents should be engaging them because they should be engaging them only when they see roads being built in their locality. Respondent –*Senator two expressed the same as Senator one.*

4.3.5. What is the Electorate's knowledge of the passage of a law by the Legislature?

Ans: Respondent-*legislator three* answered No. Respondent *legislator two* categorically said No. he further emphasized that that is the executive's responsibility. The executive should carry out awareness and sensitization on legislation debated and signed into law. Respondent Senator –Three said the electorates don't know laws passed by the house because the lack of information and awareness about the happenings in the Legislature impedes that process. Respondent-*Senator one* lamented that very few people know about the law's passage by the legislature while the majority don't know about the course of the law. Respondent-*legislator two* don't know about the path of the law in the House. Most of them don't care what happens.

4.3.6. What is the source of information used by the Legislature to publish news as it relates to the working of the Legislature?

Ans.: Respondent *legislator- one* said the National Legislature does not have any public website or library to publicize their functions and activities in the Legislature. According to respondent-*legislator two*, this is one of the challenges the Liberian legislature faces. There is a need for it to be in place. According to respondent-*legislator three*, technology is becoming more integrated into every aspect of life. As such, the legislature should now begin to have a webpage and a bulletin board to disseminate the needed information to the public, especially their constituents, so that they can know their workings and activities at the Capitol. In addition to that, respondent-*legislator four* said that there are many challenges facing the legislature and among them is the method of releasing information and out there to their people; she further emphasized that due to the large population of uneducated constituents and electorates, there is a need for some of what they do at the House to be disseminated in the local vernaculars. Respondent-legislator five said that there is no public website and bulletin for news from the House to be adequately triggered to their fellow citizens, especially their constituents.

4.4. Discussion of the Findings

This study section discusses and highlights the research findings with the 5 Respondent-Legislators. The study revealed that the population of the study was 102 members of the national legislature in domicile at the Capitol Building on Capitol Hill, Monrovia. The study highlights that those 30 senators representing 15 counties and 72 members of the Lower House are called representatives. The study sampled about 5 participants purposively from the 102 members. The five participants interviewed were from Montserrado, Sinoe, Gbarpolu, Grand Bassa, and Maryland. The research Participants had two female lawmakers, one from the senate and the other from the House of Representatives. The other three research Participants were male: two Senators and one member of the House of Representatives.

For the research questions asked about what the electorate expects from their lawmakers, most of the respondent-legislators nothing much because, according to some of them, their constituents know that much comes from the executive branch of Government while their legislators are only there to make laws. On the question of what the electorate level of participation or involvement in the passage of Bills at the Legislature, the majority of the participants answered that their constituents do not participate except where they sometimes form partnerships or come under the umbrella of civil society organizations to lobby with their Representatives to pass a bill that has a bearing on development in their district or county. On the question of how the engagement of citizens with their lawmakers during legislative recess in their various constituencies to know and understand the legislative working of the legislature, the majority of the legislator-respondents said that they are on course with their people. Most of the legislator respondents answered that they keep records on the record-keeping of their minutes and deliberations at the legislature. Still, it is done manually because there are no digital means for storage.

On the issue of electorates knowing laws passed by the legislature, the majority of the participants said no because the electorates are not interested in this process; what they are interested in is the implementation of the laws by the executive branch of government. It was also found that people attend meetings based on their interests. That is what is in there for them.

CHAPTER FIVE.

SUMMARY CONCLUSION AND RECOMMENDATIONS

5.1. Introduction

This chapter contains the summary, conclusion, and recommendations of the research. A qualitative research method was carried out, and the objective of this study was to know about the involvement of the electorates in the decision-making and legislative activities of the national legislature.

5.2. Summary

Liberia's political system has always faced severe political crises of governance and the involvement of the people. When the freemen of color meant the Americo-Liberians were brought to this land, participation in government was based on skin color, sex, gender, and identity. This system of segregation was borrowed from the design of slavery that the free slaves were accustomed to. In the ages of slavery, dark-skinned settlers worked on the plantations of the enslavers. At the same time, many emulators were children of the enslavers who were with domestic enslaved people. This identity problem contributed to the deeply rooted division between the Americo –Liberians which included the dark-skinned and the emulators that contributed to the killing of a Liberian President, Edward James Roye, by the Republican Mob dominated by the emulators.

Upon its ascendancy to power, the True Whig Party was dominantly dark-skinned but failed to correct the ills of the political system. It controlled political power for more than 133 years of the one-party system, thereby repeating the past. Political participation is an old age problem in Liberia's Political governance, meaning the total involvements of the people of Liberia have not been involved in management. In substance, some of the particular groups of people who were excluded from power and participation were the indigenous Liberians. Indigenous Liberians did not have the opportunity to participate in elections and decision-making because of segregation. This practice of 133 years of a one-party system had been systematized in all of the political structures of Liberia. Mainly, the three branches of government, Legislature, Executive, and Judiciary, were structured and designed to benefit a few individuals at the exclusion of the majority underprivileged. The system's failure to include all Liberians in the decision-making process led to one bloody coup in Liberian history led by Master Sergeant Samuel K. Doe.

On April 12, 1980, a military regime of 17 enlisted men of the Armed Forces of Liberia overthrew the President of Liberia, Dr. William R. Tolbert, Jr. This military takeover led to one of the worst experiences in Liberia. In addition to President Tolbert, 13 men who served as first circles of advisers to the President, meaning cabinet ministers and other senior members of the government of Liberia, were publicly killed on firing squad at the Barclay Training Center in Monrovia. This was the introduction of guns to solve political problems in Liberia. President Doe also did not live up to the promises of the reasons for his revolution but repeated the same mistakes of participation and included another variable in the Liberian body politics: tribalism. This variable of tribalism ushered in a strange tension between two Liberian tribes, the Gio, Mano of one side from Nimba County, and the Krahn from Grand Gedeh. Consequently, the decade of rule by President Samuel K. Doe ended with the introduction of the famous people uprising headed by President Charles G. Taylor.

The Popular people's uprising lasted for fourteen (14) years of civil war, which claimed over 250,000 lives and destroyed almost all of Liberia's infrastructures. During the Liberian Civil War, several cases of abuse ranged from rape, extermination, or killings (murder), abduction, forceful recruitment of child soldiers, and other violations of international humanitarian law and criminal law. These atrocities caused the establishment of a Truth and Reconciliation Commission (TRC) in Liberia to investigate the causes and antecedents of the Liberian conflict. The truth commission completed its mandate and recommended, and amongst those recommendations and identifications of the causes and antecedents of the Liberian Conflict was the "absence and exclusions of a significant of Liberians from political participation in government. The conflicts' causes are categorized into immediate and remote causes, antecedents, and U.S Relations with Liberia.

With the transition of Liberia from the period of the Civil War to a democratic society, Liberia became the first country in Africa to produce a woman as President of Liberia, Madam Ellen Johnson Sirleaf. Upon her ascendancy as President of Liberia, President Sirleaf received numerous support to build Liberia on the path of democratization. Much of Madam Ellen Johnson's license from the international community was intended to foster support for political inclusion in governance and encourage women's participation. The Sirleaf government received the support of up to 5 billion from the United States Government, with some focus on "House Democracy Partnership with the Liberian Legislature." In all of the periods of leadership under Madam Ellen Johnson Sirleaf, the issue of electorate participation which includes knowledge of the legislature functions, responsibilities, and accountability, had been a significant challenge in the Liberia democracy. Some of the reasons responsible for the limited if not lack of involvement of the people in the legislative decision-making process can be attributed to i) lack of knowledge, ii) no interest in the electorate due to irresponsible leadership that has frustrated the electorates, iii) lack of political will on the part of political leaders to be accountable, iv) lack of public information system and technology available for the people, and v) poverty.

Political participation is directly related to economic development. Participation allows tapping into many skills and individual contributions of citizens who will contribute to the nation-building process. Participation allows for people of all kinds, including women, males, children, and all persons from all walks of life. Liberia, from time immemorial, had not been able to capitalize on this golden opportunity of participation. At the national Legislature, with all of the support to democratize Liberia, the involvement of the electorates in the Legislative process remains a challenge for the Liberian democracy.

In the legacy of Liberia, governance has always been conducted at the exclusion of the governed. The culture of exclusion has been systemic in almost all branches of government, especially the national legislature, which is no exception. One can sum this to be a crisis of participation which is a significant factor in the Liberian conflict. The findings of this research support this in that the first branch of Government (national legislature) also does not include the involvement of the people in the decision-making process; this has caused the electorate to lack basic knowledge of their responsibilities in the legislative process. The legislature lacks the forum to educate and allow participation of the citizens in that the electorates even if a particular representative calls an individual meeting, questions that are asked regarding responsibilities which should be attributed to the executive branch for answers are referred to the Legislature, as such the citizens lack the benchmark to judge a particular legislator regarding their functions as the Representative. In essence, the electorates are not involved in the decision-making process at the legislature.

5.3. Conclusion

There is a lack of a system or structure that informs, educates, and directs electorates about the questions that need to be asked in their specific roles in the national legislative functions of Liberia. As a result, the majority of the citizens of Liberia do not know what is required of a legislator to discharge their roles and how the parts of the Legislation directly affect the citizens. So participation is a major crisis in our democracy.

Until an educational forum is developed at the level of the legislature, access to the legislative library is digitized, and public, academic conferences are created to better inform the citizens of what is expected of them in the representative democracy, participation is a significant problem for the Liberian public. Also, this will require that standards are developed and promulgated to allow adequate public participation in the formulation and promulgation of law at the legislature to improve the governance at the legislative level, meaning that legislators are aware that they are consciously held accountable by the electorates based on standards and performances as well as results.

The research has shown that the electorates are not fully aware of what is expected of their lawmakers, even to the extent that in all engagements with their legislators, they ask questions unrelated to legislative functions that will impact their lives. This is because electorates do not know what is expected of a Legislator and the electorates are not generally involved in the decision-making process at the Legislature. As a result, they do not know the bills passed by their Representatives and what impact those laws have on them.

If an individual Lawmaker makes any attempt to call meetings during recess, it is based on the Legislator of an individual Lawmaker's attempts to call meetings during the break; it is based on the Legislator's will. Generally, Lawmakers will only allow contact for constituency meetings when they have a particular political interest in a specific issue. The involvement of the people is a significant challenge in policy decisions in the Legislature. Therefore, emphasis must be directed by political leaders to allow for more participation of the people in the Legislative process.

5.4. Recommendations

As the result of the findings of this study, the researcher recommends the following:

1. There is a need for a public bulletin (website) to be called the public library of the national legislature that will educate Liberian citizens or the electorate about the roles of their Legislators and what is expected of them.
2. There should be a policy requiring public debate or hearings on all bills intended to be passed by the national legislature into law. This must require that a Bill should be deliberated not less than six months before it is passed into law. This

will enable more education and awareness of the bill intended to be passed into law so that the electorates will know what is intended of them.

3. The recording of the minutes of the legislature should graduate from a manual to a computerized system for accessibility purposes.
4. There is a need for public education for a national policy for the electorate to know what precisely they are required to ascertain from their legislators after being elected to the House.
5. The government of Liberia should go a step further from the proceedings of the passage of a bill by the legislature to the signing by the President into handbills and the official gazette. That is to say; the GOL should employ civic education of every law in making sure that the citizens are aware and understand the nature and extent of the law passed so that they can appreciate whether the law is within the moral sentiment of their community that is intended to be served or affected. This involves using other civil society organizations or the ministry of information, radio programs, workshops, newspaper publications, websites, etc.
6. The passage of a bill in the Legislature must encourage public debates and discussions on the legislation; allow members of the electorates to deliberate on the bill before the course. This will demonstrate and identify whether or not the intended bill meets the popular support of the people.
7. A standard should be established that requires the recording of votes by members of the Legislature on bills and decisions taken by members of the first branch of government. This will also require public knowledge to be available on a Legislative website, giving access to public views about the deliberations and votes in the Legislature, including other information on the Legislative Process.
8. The Legislature should be regarded as the people's House and have the right to know what is going on and what needs to happen, thereby directing they're elected what they want.
9. Women participation in Legislative politics is wanting and should be encouraged.

5.5 Future Research

This study advises that there should be more research in the following areas to foster and provide support and guidance in citizens' participation in governance:

1. A study needs to be done on whether there are legislative recordings and coding of legislative minutes of bills passed by the national legislature to provide an

understanding of the legislative history of the laws passed by the National Legislature for research purposes.

2. There is also a need to conduct future studies on how bills are passed into law by the legislature and how they affect the lives of the people of Liberia, particularly the electorates. This must be followed by knowing what sector of the nation is affected and the benefits and implementation of these laws. It also follows that an inquiry should be made on the process of public involvement in the passage of the laws: deliberation process of the enactment of the law, who is involved.

3. Study also needs to be done on the level of civil society involvement in the passage of the law.

REFERENCES

Adam, P, Susan C. Stokes, and Bernard, M, (1999). eds., *Democracy, Accountability and Representation* New York: Cambridge University Press.

Atul, K, (1986). "Democracy and Development," in *Development Strategies Reconsidered*, ed. *John Lewis and Valeriana Kallab New Brunswick, NJ: Transaction Books, p. 153.*

Alexis de T, (1961). *Democracy in America*, ed. J. P. Mayer and Max Lerner New York: Harper and Row,

Arend. L, (1984). *Democracies: Patterns of Majoritarian and Consensus Government in Twenty One Countries* (New Haven, CT: Yale University Press.

An Act to Grant Immunity from Both Civil and Criminal Proceedings Against all Persons within the Jurisdiction of the Republic of Liberia from Acts and or Crimes Committed During the Civil War from December 1989 to August 2003.

Andrei .S (1993), *"Corruption," Quarterly Journal of Economics* 108, no.3: 599-617.

Andrimihaja, C, (2011). *"Avoiding the Fragility Trap in Africa," Policy Research Paper 5884, The World Bank.*

Anke, H, (2004). *Greed and Grievance in Civil War*, Oxford Economic Papers 50 (4):563- 95.

Anderson, J. (2004), "Trade Costs," *Journal of Economic Literature*, Vol. 42, pp. 691-751.

Azango, B (1971). *"The Present Socio-Economic Situation in Liberia and Its Implications for the Educational System."* Liberian Research Association Journal 6, No.3: 1-34.

Baldwin, R., "21st Century Regionalism: *Filling the Gap between 21st Century Trade and 20th Century Trade Rules", Graduate Institute*, Geneva, April 2011.

Barkey, R (1967). *"National Accounting with Limited Data: Lessons from Liberia."* Paper Read at a conference of the Harvard D.A.S. at Sorrento, September.

Blamo, J. (1971). *"Nation-Building in Liberia: The Use of Symbols in National Integration.* Liberian Studies Journal 4, no.1: 21-30.

Blattman, C., and Edward, M, (2010). *"Civil War," Journal of Economic Literature*, Vol. 48, No.1, pp. 3-57.

Boas, M. (2001). *"Liberia and Sierra Leone: Dead Ringers? The Logic of Neo-patrimonial Rule", Third World Quarterly*, Vol. 22, No.5, pp. 697-723.

Brooks, and Douglas H. (2008), *"Regional Cooperation, Infrastructure, and Trade Costs in Asia,"* Asian Development Working Paper, No. 123.

Brown and George W. (1941). *The Economic History of Liberia. Washington, D.C.*: Associated Publishers.

Cette, G., and Jimmy L, (2009), *"ICT Demand Behavior: An International Comparison," Banque de France* Working Paper No.252.

Clower, R, (1966). *Growth without Development: An Economic Survey of Liberia Evanston*: Northwestern University Press.

Coale, W, (1978). *West German Transnationals in Africa*: The case of Liberia and the Bong Mining Company. *Munich: Info-Institut fur Wirtschftsforschung-Welform Verlag.*

Cole, and Robert E. (1967). *"The Liberian Elite as a Barrier to Economic Development." Ph.D. Dissertation, Department of Economics*, Northwestern University, Evanston, Ill.

Congressional Research Service (CRS) Report. (2023). In Focus Liberia. Available at: https://www.everycrsreport.com/files/2023-09-15_IF12493_8b7d4a21ab5ef5d5ccc68c7196e5443516eb641e.pdf

Constitution of the Republic of Liberia, 1986.

David S. (2005), *"Democracy and Education Spending in Africa," American Journal of Political Science* 49, no. 2: 343-358.

David, K. (2002), *Crony Capitalism: Corruption and Development in South Korea and the Philippines* (New York: Cambridge University Press).

Dawn, B. (2006). "*Decentralization: Fueling the Fire or Dampening the Flames of Ethnic Conflict and Secessionism,*" *International Security* 60, no. 3: 651-685.

Dalton, G. (1965). "*History, Politics and Economic Development in Liberia.*" Journal of Economic History 25 (Dec):569-91.

Deutsche, G. (2011). *Capacity Development for the Transport Sector in Liberia*" The Transport Master Plan of Liberia.

Dunn, D. (1988). *Liberia: A Polity in Transition. Metuchen*, NJ: Scarecrow Press.

Dwan, R, (May 2006). "*Liberia's Governance and Economic Management Assistance Program (GEMAP): A joint review by the Department of Peacekeeping Best* Practices Section and the World Bank's Fragile States Group".

Eleanor, O, (1990). *Governing the Commons: The Evolution of Institutions for Collective Action* (New York: Cambridge University Press).

Egert, B, (2009). "*Infrastructure and Growth: Empirical Evidence," Economics Department Working Paper No. 685, OECD, Paris.*"Education Sector Plan for Liberia: Commitment to Make a Difference."

FEWSNET and USAID, (2010). "*Cross Border Trade and Food Security: Liberia and Sierra Leone*".

Friedman, J. (1974) "*The Absorption of Labor in an Urban Economy: The Case of Developing Economies,*" Economic Development and Cultural Change, Vol. 22, No.3 pp. 385-413.

Fareed, Z, (2004). "*Islam, Democracy and Constitutional Liberalism,*" *Political Science Quarterly* 119, no. 1: 2.

Francis F, (2004). "*The Imperative of State-Building,*" *Journal of Democracy* 15, no. 2 17-31.

Geterminah, H.N. (2021). Advocates call on UN to set up war in Liberia. Daily Observer Online. Published 7/20/2021 -12:06. Available at : https://www.liberianobserver.com/advocates call-un-set-war-court liberia#:~:text=The%20President%20of%20the%20Liberia,economic%20crimes%20court%20for%20Liberia.

Gockowski, J., (2010). *"Intensified Cocoa for Sustainable Development in Liberia,"* mimeo. The University of Tennessee.

Guannu. (2010). *A short history of the first Liberian republic, (3rd Edition).* Star Books.

Guannu, J. S. (2010). *Liberia history up to 1847.* 325. Exposition Press Inc.

Holloway, J. S. (1981). *Confronting the veil: Abram Harris, Jr., E. Franklin Frazier, and Ralph Bunche, 1919-1941.* University of North Carolina Press.

International Institute of Tropical Agriculture, (2008). *"Reforming Cocoa and Coffee Marketing in Liberia,"* Policy Brief, No. 2,

John C, (1991). *Democratizing Development: The Role of Voluntary Organizations* and Alfred Montero and David Samuels, eds., *Decentralization and Democracy in Latin America* (Notre Dame, IN: University of Notre Dame Press, 2004).

Jonathan R, (2002). "*The Dilemma of Fiscal Federalism:* Grants and Fiscal Performance around The World," *American Journal of Political Science* 46, no. 3: 670-687.

Kathleen O, (2005). *Decentralizing the State: Elections, Parties and Local Power in the Andes* (New York: Cambridge University Press.

Kaba, B. (2006), "*On Some Aspects Of The Current State Of The Liberian Economy*: A Tentative Diagnostic And Assessment".

Kangou, S, (2005), *"Civil War Destruction and the Prospects for Economic Growth,"* *The Journal of Politics,* Vol. 67, No. 1, pp. 68-109.

Keili, F. (2008). "*Small Arms and Light Weapons Transfer in West Africa: A Stock-taking," Disarmament Forum,* No. 4, pp. 6-11.

Koinyeneh, G.C.(2021). Liberian Bar Association's President calls on United Nations Security Council to establish war and economic crimes court for Liberia. Front Page Africa online, Published July 20, 2021. Available at: https://frontpageafricaonline.com/liberia-war crimes-trial/liberian-bar-associations-president-calls-on-united-nations-security-council-to-establish-war-economic-crimes-court-for-liberia/

Liberia Ministry of Agriculture, "Liberia Agricultural Sector Investment Program," May 2010.

Malac, D.R. (2015). The latest chapter in US-Liberia relations. Available at: https://s3.amazonaws.com/caa-production/attachments/511/C_Pages24to26_Malac.pdf?1428599453

Ministry of Planning and Economic Affairs and UNDP, (2011)*"Liberia National Capacity Development Strategy.*

Ministry of Gender Development and World Bank, (2010). "*Gender Aware Programs and Women's Roles in Agricultural Value Chains*: A Policy Memorandum.

Moore Stephens, "*Report on the Third LEITI Reconciliation Exercise*, Covering the Period July 1, 2009, to June 30, 2010.

North, D. (1990). *Institutions, Institutional Change and Economic Performance.* Cambridge University Press.

National Elections Commission of Liberia (NEC), United Nations Development Programme, UN Women Liberia.(2023). Public perceptions about elections and women political participation in Liberia. https://www.undp.org/sites/g/files/zskgke326/files/2023-05/PUBLIC%20PERCEPTIONS%20OF%20ELECTIONS%20AND%20WOMEN%20POLITICAL%20PARTICIPATION%20IN%20LIBERIA.pdf

Okolo, J. (1989). "Obstacles to Increased Intra-Ecowas Trade," International Journal, Vol. 44, No. 1, pp. 171-214.

Outram, Q. (1999). "Liberia: Roots and Fruits of the Emergency, Third World Quarterly, Vol. 20, No. 1, pp. 163-173.

Patrick Heller, "Moving the State: The Politics of Democratic Decentralization in Kerala, South Africa, and Porto Alegre," *Politics and Society* 29, no. 1 (March 2001): 131-163.

Philip Oxhorn, Joseph Tulchin, and Andrew Selee, eds., *Decentralization, Democratic Governance and Civil Society in Comparative Perspective: Africa, Asia and Latin America* (Washington, DC: Woodrow Wilson Center Press, 2004).

Republic of Liberia Ministry of Education, "Education Sector Plan for Liberia: Commitment to Make a Difference."

Republic of Liberia Ministry of Planning and Economic Affairs, (2011). "*Developing Liberia's Economic Corridors, Volumes 1 and 2*".

Riley, S., and Max S, (1996). "*Liberia: after Abuja," Review of African Political Economy*" pp. 429-437.

Roughton International, Regional Road Transport and Transit Facilitation Programme in West Africa, Volume I Final Report, June 2006.

Robert B, (1996). *Getting It Right: Markets and Choices in a Free Society* (Cambridge, MA: MIT Press.

Rob J, (1999). *Democratic Politics and Economic Reform in India* (New York: Cambridge University Press.

Robert J, (1990). *Quasi-States: Sovereignty, International Relations and the Third World* (New York: Cambridge University Press, 155-183.

Robert W, (1987). *Village Republics: Economic Conditions for Collective Action in South India* (New York: Cambridge University Press,

Remy P', (1995). "The Dangers of Decentralization," *World Bank Research Observer* 10, no. 2: 201-220.

Schroeder, G. (2006). *"The Illicit Arms Trade in Africa: A Global Enterprise, African Analyst*, Third Quarter, pp. 69-78.

Stohl, R, (2005). "*Fighting the Illicit Trafficking of Small Arms," SAIS Review*, Winter/Spring 2 Edition, pp. 1-9.

Stephan H, and Robert K, (1995). *The Political Economy of Democratic Transitions* (Princeton, NJ: Princeton University Press).

Samuel H, (1991). *The Third Wave: Democratization in the Late Twentieth Century* (Norman, OK: University of Oklahoma Press).

Samuel H, (1968). *Political Order in Changing Societies* (New Haven, CT: Yale University Press).

Tefft, J. (2005*), Agricultural Policy and Food Security in Liberia,* ESA Paper, FAO Regional Office for Africa.

The World Bank. (2023). The World Bank in Liberia: Liberia's poverty reduction strategy is supported by the rebuilding of core functions and institutions, rehabilitating infrastructures, and facilitating growth. Available at: https://www.worldbank.org/en/country/liberia/overview

Tsimpo, C and Wodon, Q. (2012). *Rice Prices and Poverty in Liberia," included in Poverty and the Policy Response to the Economic Crisis in Liberia*, The World Bank.

UNDP, Human Development Report (2003), Millennium Development Goals: *A compact among nations to end human poverty.*

Vito T, (2000). "*On Fiscal Federalism: Issues to Worry About," paper presented at the IMF Conference on Fiscal Decentralization*, Washington, DC,

Vamvakidis, A., (1998). "*Regional Integration and Economic Growth,"* The World Bank Review, Vol. 12, pp. 251-270.

Wander, H., (1986). "*Population, Labor Supply, and Employment in Developing Countries,"* Annals of the American Academy of Political and Social Science, Vol. 492 pp. 69-79.

Wallace O, (1972). *Fiscal Federalism* (New York: Harcourt, Brace, and Jovanovich).

West Africa Mineral Sector Strategic Assessment (2010): *An Environmental and Social Strategic Assessment for Mano River Union,* The World Bank Report No. 53738.

Wilcox, M., (2010). "*Reforming Cocoa and Coffee Marketing in Liberia,"* Mimeograph, University of Tennessee, www.napu.edu (1992) Democratization in Africa: African Views: African Voices National Academics of Sciences, Engineering, and Medicine.

Woods, N. (1999). Good governance in international organizations. *Global Governance*, Jan.–Mar. 1999, Vol. 5, No. 1 (Jan.–Mar. 1999), pp. 39-61

Wi Williams v Tah et al [2011] LRSC 12 (21 January 2011); Available at: http://www.liberlii.org/lr/cases/LRSC/2011/12.html

APPENDIX

Thesis Topic: An Inquiry into People's Participation in Legislative Workings in Their Constituencies: Case Study of The National Legislature (2006-2012)

A. Demographic Profile of Respondents

1. Gender of Respondents: Female ( ) Male ( )
2. Age Range of Respondents: 18-25 ( ) 26-35 ( ) 36-45 ( ) 46-Above ( )
3. Educational Level of Respondents: High School Graduate ( ) College Student ( ) Bachelor Degree Holder ( ) Masters Student ( ) Masters' Degree Holder ( )
4. Doctor ( ) Others ( )
5. Marital Status of respondents Single ( ) Engaged ( ) Married ( ) Separated ( ) Divorced ( ) Widow ( ) Widower ( )
6. County of Origin:
7. Maryland ( ) Montserrado ( ) Bong ( ) Margibi ( ) Sinoe ( ) River Gee ( ) Grand Bassa ( ) Rivercess ( ) Bomi ( ) Nimba ( ) Grand Gedeh ( ) Cape Mount ( ) Grand Kru ( ) Gbarpolu ( ) Lofa ( )
8. Position/title/ rank of respondents
9. Senator ( ) Representative ( )
10. Length of Time At The Legislature: 0-6 years ( ) 7-12 years ( ) 130-18 years ()

B. Open Ended Interview Questions With The Participants

1. What Does the Electorate expect of their lawmaker?

   ____

2. What Are the Electorate's Level of Participation or Involvement in the Passage of Bills at the National Legislation?

   ____

3. How is the record-keeping Process at The National Legislation in Recording Minutes of Deliberations on the Passage of Bills for Future Reference?

   ____

4. How Are the Citizens Engagement with Their Legislators during Legislative Recess In Their Various Constituencies to know and understand the Legislative Working of the Legislators?

____

5. What Is the Electorate Knowledge on the Passage of Law By the Legislature?

____

6. What is the Source of Information Used by the Legislature to Publish Information as it Relates to the Working of the Legislature?

____

C. Thesis Topic: An Inquiry into People's Participation in Legislative Workings in Their Constituencies: Case Study of The National Legislature (2006-2012)

Demographic Profile of Respondents

1. Gender of Respondents: Female ( ) Male ( )
2. Age Range of Respondents : 18-25 ( ) 26-35 ( ) 36-45 ( ) 46-Above ( )
3. Educational Level of Respondents : High School Graduate ( ) College Student ( ) Bachelor Degree Holder ( ) Masters Student ( ) Masters' Degree Holder ( ) Doctor ( ) Others ( )
4. Marital Status of respondents Single ( ) Engaged ( ) Married ( ) Separated ( ) Divorced ( ) Widow ( ) Widower ( )
5. County of Origin:
   Maryland ( ) Montserrado ( ) Bong ( ) Margibi ( ) Sinoe ( ) River Gee ( ) Grand Bassa ( ) Rivercess ( ) Bomi ( ) Nimba ( ) Grand Gedeh ( ) Cape Mount ( ) Grand Kru ( ) Gbarpolu ( ) Lofa ( )
6. Position/title/ rank of respondents
   Senator ( ) Representative ( )
7. Length of Time At The Legislature: 0-6 years ( ) 7-12 years( ) 130-18 years ( )

Open-Ended Interview Questions with the Participants

1. What Does the Electorate expect of their lawmaker?

___

2. What Are the Electorate Level of Participation or Involvement in the Passage of Bills at the National Legislation?

___

3. How is the record-keeping Process at The National Legislation in Recording Minutes of Deliberations on the Passage of Bills for Future Reference?

___

4. How Are the Citizens Engagement with Their Legislators during Legislative Recess In Their Various Constituencies to know and understand the Legislative Working of the Legislators?

___

5. What Are the Electorates' Knowledge of the Passage of Law By the Legislature?

___

6. What is the Source of Information Used by the Legislature to Publish Information as it Relates to the Working of the Legislature?

___

Thanks So Much for Participating in This Research!

www.ingramcontent.com/pod-product-compliance
Lightning Source LLC
LaVergne TN
LVHW022315200926
848481LV00004B/1349